IN HIS HAND

IN HIS HAND

Part 1

Graydon F. Snyder
Associate Professor of Biblical Studies
Bethany Theological Seminary

CHURCH OF THE BRETHREN
SENIOR HIGH YOUTH CURRICULUM

Editors

Richard H. Coffman, editor of youth publications
Ercell V. Lynn, editor of Christian education publications
Ora W. Garber, editor of book publications

Consultant

Joseph M. Long, director of youth work

Cover by Harry Durkee

IN HIS HAND, Part 1, copyright 1964 by General Brotherhood Board, Church of the Brethren, Elgin, Illinois

All biblical material, unless otherwise indicated, is taken from the Revised Standard Version of the Bible, copyrighted 1946 and 1952 by the National Council of Churches of Christ in the U. S. A. and used by permission.

The senior high youth curriculum provides three areas of study:

In his hand, a comprehensive, yearlong survey of the Bible, is designed to give youth an overall understanding of biblical history and content.

In Christ Jesus consists of a six-month study of the significance and reality of Christ, a three-month unit designed to help youth develop an understanding of themselves in relationship with God and others, and a three-month study of the meaning of discipleship.

In his Spirit is a yearlong, four-part study of the implications of giving God one's supreme loyalty, the nature of freedom and responsibility, the nature of the church, and the ministry of reconciliation.

What is God trying to say to me?

Soren Kierkegaard, the Danish philosopher, tells of a young man who received a lengthy letter from his girlfriend. As it happened, she was of a different nationality and wrote to him in her own language. He had a speaking acquaintance with that language, but was hardly an expert. As he tried to read the letter he could understand that she was coming to visit him and wanted him to take care of several things before she arrived. He was not absolutely certain what she wanted done, but he knew it was important and that she would be coming soon. He was faced with a dilemma: Should he borrow some dictionaries and try to translate the letter word for word, or should he start immediately to do as much as he could understand from the letter?

What would you do? What would make his girl happier — a translation of the letter or a simple statement, "I'm not sure of everything you said, but I did what I could"? Clearly, loyalty to the beloved means action even if the wishes are not fully understood.

We do not fully understand the Bible. We never will. But here it is, full of urgent requests from One who loves us. We could argue and debate the meanings of each passage. But the time is short. The world doesn't wait. Let us do the best we can, take what we have, and run with all our might!

This book examines the meaning of the Bible. In the microviews I have tried to tell what selected passages mean to me. You could ask me many questions: "Do you have a correct understanding? Why did you choose certain passages for study?" These may be good questions and you may be justified in asking them. But this is a plea to take what you can get and live on the basis of that. Don't fight with me. Read the Bible yourself and ask: "What is God trying to say to *me*?"

It is reported that Mark Twain was talking with a well-meaning Christian woman who said, "The thing that bothers me about the Bible is that there is so much I can't understand." Mark Twain replied, "Madam, it is not what I don't understand that bothers me. It's what I *do* understand!"

1

In the beginning

OVERVIEW 1
Genesis 1 — 11

The Hebrew people were not especially interested in the "how" or even the "what" of life, the world, and history. But they continually asked, "Why?"

Why did God create the world?
Why am I here?
Why am I like I am?
Why do I want to do this or that, but always foul it up?
Why doesn't God give up with man?
Why were *we* chosen to serve him?
Why do we have to be different?

The answers to these questions are found in Genesis, especially the first eleven chapters. Without this prologue the Bible would make little sense. We can say this for two reasons:

1. The history and the literature we are about to study (from Genesis 12 to The Revelation to John) are not simply an ancient history about a special group of people. The Bible is a book for all people and the story we find there is for all men. Genesis 1 – 11 shows why God's concern for man came to focus on a given people (the descendants of Abraham). Without this understanding, the Jews will look like a crazy people with a God-complex.

2. The Bible is not only historical but it is also personal. It is a long history of God's making himself known to man, *but it is also the story of our life.* Genesis 1 – 11 makes this clear. *Adam* (Hebrew word meaning mankind) is literally *every man* and this is the story of each of us at birth, in our childhood, in our youth, at maturity, and finally in death itself. It is important that we not forget this, lest we read the Bible as if it had nothing to do with us.

As you read in Genesis you will discover that there are apparent duplications. There seem to be two stories of creation (1:1 – 2:4a and 2:4b – 2:24), two distinct accounts of the creation of man and woman (1:26f. and 2:7, 22), and two accounts of the flood intertwined (compare 7:2-4 with 7:15f.). Observance of this fact can be of considerable aid in understanding the nature of the Bible and how it came to us. Most of the Pentateuch (the first five books of the Old Testament) and much of the Former Prophets (Joshua, Judges, 1 and 2 Samuel, 1 and 2 Kings) is composed of various strands of tradition.

In the case of the Pentateuch there was an early tradition formulated when the tribes first came together in Palestine. This tradition was used in the worship and the teaching of Israel for many centuries and by different groups. From time to time the tradition was expressed in a permanent form — either written or oral and usually because of some need or crisis among the Hebrew people. These permanent expressions differed from one another, yet depended on one another, so that the Old Testament as we now have it contains parts of all these expressions of the tradition. After considerable study we have come to the conclusion that in the Pentateuch four expressions of the same tradition make up the final version as we know it. We identify these four expressions according to the periods in which they originated:

1. The Jahwist (J) used the name *Lord* (*Jahweh*) for God and wrote his version of the tradition during the time of David.
2. The Elohist (E) used *God* (*Elohim*) as the name for the divine being and he (or they) expressed this version of the tradition during the height of the northern prophetic movement.
3. The Deuteronomist (D) especially emphasizes the covenant element of the tradition for the later years of the southern kingdom.
4. The Priestly writer (P) presents the tradition as a guide for the Jewish community which returned from Babylonia. Put in graphic form, it might look like this:

	1000	900	800	700	600	500	400 B.C.
ORAL TRADITION		J			JE		
			E		D		JEDP
						P	

When we find duplications or seeming contradictions in this part of the Old Testament we should be aware that there are several expressions of the same tradition involved. And the question is not which is correct or which is the oldest, but rather why the final tradition retained both expressions.

Sabbath signifies perfect fellowship

Before we take a closer look at some of the stories in Genesis 1 — 11, let us consider the total section. It starts with a majestic statement of God's creation of the universe (1:1 — 2:4a, P). This section ends with the seventh day, a day which signifies the perfect fellowship between man, God, and the world. This "rest" is described here by a second creation story (2:4b — 2:24, J), which stresses the relation of man to the world which God created.

In chapter 3 we discover how it is that man comes to rebel against God and to distrust his fellowman — in other words, the origin of sin. The implications of this for the family, the nation, and history itself are spelled out in chapter 4.

Chapter 5 (P) shows that there is another side of Adam. God raises up from Seth a people who "call upon the name of the Lord" and from this family arise Abraham, Israel, and ultimately the church.

But it is not simply a matter that some people are good and some are bad. Because of man's distrust, the entire created universe is "fouled up" (6:1-4). **God is** sorry he has made such a mess and threatens to destroy creation by returning it to the primeval watery chaos (6:5 — 9:19), but in his mercy he saves Noah and his family along with the animals. God promises Noah never again to destroy mankind as a means of solving the problems of sin. Good as Noah was, he and his family were far from perfect (9:20-28), and chapter 10 describes how the family of Noah, both good and evil, formed the Near Eastern civilization.

Now it is man's turn to try to solve the situation. He builds a tower to heaven so as to become like God (11:1-9). It is a false solution. To prevent man from finding satisfaction in vain hopes, God divides man into linguistic groups so that communication between man becomes impossible. The remainder of chapter 11 describes the origin of Abraham from Shem (hence the name *Semites*).

A closer look at three stories in Genesis 1 – 11 will especially help us understand what the biblical faith is about man and his world. In the first story, 1:1-25, we shall discover what the Hebrew believed about the world in which he lived. A second set of stories describes the nature of man and his relationship to others, found in 1:26-31 and 2:18-23. Most important, of course, is the description of man's fall as found in Genesis 3:1-11. Let's look at them.

Fact or fiction?

MICROVIEW 1a
Genesis 1:1-25

The Bible comes right to the point. "In the beginning *God* created the heavens and the earth." No wasted words, no apology — God did it. All of it. And how did God accomplish this tremendous action? Simply by saying the word. No dirty hands, no sweating muscles — God just spoke.

The order is interesting, too. First he separated night from day (vv. 3-5). Next he made a sky (firmament) to separate the water of the heavens (rain) from the water of the earth (vv. 6-8). Then he separated the ground from the water on earth (vv. 9f.). After this he planted all vegetation which can be found around the world (vv. 11-13) and then he put the sun, the moon, and the stars in the sky as a sign of the difference between day and night (vv. 14-19). Without pausing for even a second breath, God goes on to make all the animals, birds, and fish which inhabit the earth (vv. 20-25) and as the apex of his work he makes him who shall have dominion over all the world: man. All of this in six days!

In this world dominated by scientific achievement even the most casual reader will have questions about this account of creation. He has learned that the sun gives us light and daytime and that it was in the sky long before the earth was created. He is aware of the long, long time involved in the formation of the earth and the development of life; six days from a gaseous ball of fire to even primitive man remains unbelievable. Thus many persons have read the first 25 verses of the Bible

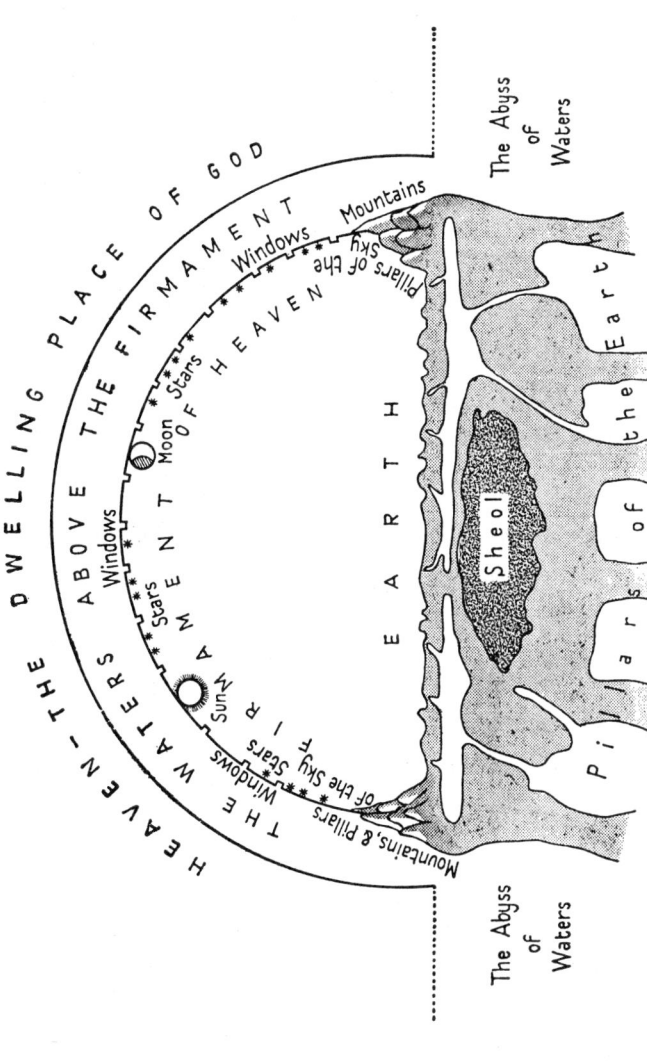

HEBREW CONCEPTION OF THE UNIVERSE

From S. H. Hooke, *In the Beginning*, Volume 6 (London: Oxford University Press, copyright 1947).

and dismissed the whole thing as so much religious "hogwash." They throw away the Bible and return to their science textbooks. Others may throw away their textbooks and say, "The Bible seems absurd, but I believe it anyway." Both of these attitudes are serious mistakes.

Two kinds of knowledge

In order to understand the creation story we must realize that there are two types of knowledge: factual and relational. *Factual knowledge* is what we know about things — how they work, of what they are made, their color, their texture, and other physical characteristics. *Relational knowledge* is the knowledge we find in personal involvement — character, thoughts, speech, and the beauty of another person. Factual knowledge can be classified, described, catalogued, and controlled. Relational knowledge is personal and cannot be classified or limited in that way.

Both of these forms of knowledge are necessary for us. In fact, they are normally so intertwined that we do not bother to separate them. For example, you may know the date of birth and the color of the eyes and the hair of your girl friend; but if this is all you know about her you would hardly "know" her. This is only factual knowledge. But if you love her and know her personally, then *what* you know about her takes on a special significance. If she has green eyes and red hair, then the sight of green eyes and red hair will always remind you of her *as a person*.

God is not measurable

Our knowledge of God is much the same. Factual

knowledge about God is meaningless apart from our personal knowledge of him. The modern reader who says he wants only "facts" has reduced life to factual knowledge and does not realize that this is not life at all. Oddly enough, the reader who claims that the Bible is entirely "factual" has done exactly the same thing. He too has reduced knowledge of God to information. But God is not measurable. He can be described, but he is not the sum of all our descriptions. God is personal and our knowledge of him is personal. *It is this knowledge or involvement with God that we call "faith."*

So when we say that "God created" we do not mean it as a scientific statement, but rather as a faith statement. This says something about the relationship of the world and man to God. It says nothing about *how* the world began. Man's idea of how the world began has changed a great deal since this passage was written and it will change in the future. But the nature of man's relationship to God and to the world in which he lives will never change. It is of this relationship that the Bible speaks.

A Babylonian faith statement

Every culture and religion has a faith statement about creation. The odd-sounding poem below, which the Hebrew people knew well, is taken from the Babylonian *Epic of Creation,* discovered in 1876. It is a "faith myth" in which Marduk represents order, growth, and good while Tiamat represents chaos and evil.

Marduk is the god of Babylon and the king of gods. He leads in battle with Tiamat — a goddess monster who is in charge of those gods who rebel against Marduk. The world is a result of the defeat of Tiamat and her dismemberment.

IV

93 So they came together — Tiamat, and Marduk, Sage of the gods:
They advanced into conflict, they joined forces in battle.
He spread wide his net, the lord, and enveloped her,
The Evil Wind, the rearmost, unleashed in her face.

97 As she opened her mouth, Tiamat to devour him,
He made the Evil Wind to enter that she closed not her lips:
The Storm Winds, the furious, then filling her belly,
Her inwards became distended, she opened fully wide her mouth.

101 He shot therethrough an arrow, it pierced her stomach,
Clave through her bowels, tore into her womb:
Thereat he strangled her, made her life-breath ebb away,
Cast her body to the ground, standing over it (in triumph).

135 He rested, the lord, examining her body:
Would divide up the monster, create a wonder of wonders!
He slit her in two like a fish of the drying yards,
The one half he positioned and secured as the sky. . . .

V

1 (Therein) traced he lines for the mighty gods,
Stars, star-groups and constellations he appointed for them:
He determined the year, marked out its divisions,
For each of the twelve months appointed three rising stars.

5 Having established the rules for the (astronomical) seasons,
He laid down the Crossing-line to make known their limits:
And that none should make mistake or in any way lose speed

He appointed, conjointly with it, the Enlil- and Ea-lines.

9 The great (Sun-) gates he opened in both sides of her ribs,
Made strong the lock-fastening to left and right:
In the depths of her belly he laid down the *elati*.
He made the moon to shine forth, entrusted to him the night.*

This poem sounds fantastic, but actually we should regard it as a statement of faith. Since chaos always threatens to disrupt the order of life, those who believe in this myth symbolize the threat in the re-enactment of the Tiamat myth annually. They do this by various means: magic, fertility rites, and other ceremonies of a natural religion. For them the world depends on the outcome of the struggle between these deities and not upon a God who creates or a man who acts responsibly.

The Hebrews knew of Tiamat. In fact, she appears as the "deep" in Genesis 1:2 (*tehom* in the Hebrew). But the Hebrews rejected the faith of Babylon. Their faith is unique. Other cultures speak of a god who would not create, but still they believe the world is an image of the divine. For them the world is not real but only a shadow. They must try to live in that real world, if they can. Others would say that the world was made of evil matter and man was only accidentally caught in it. Man must act to free himself of this prison and return to the true spiritual world.

The Hebrew faith statement

The Genesis account neatly avoids all these problems.

---

* D. Winton Thomas, editor, *Documents from Old Testament Times*, translated with introductions and notes by members of the Society for Old Testament Study (Edinburgh and London: Thomas Nelson and Sons Ltd., copyright 1958).

1. The world is made by God,
    but it is not a part of God and therefore not divine.
2. The world is made of nothing or chaos;
    therefore its origin and structure are not from something other than God.
3. The world is made by God speaking;
    therefore it is willed by him and not an accident.
4. The world is good;
    therefore the evil of the world is due to man, not to God's act of creation.

This is a great faith statement that has molded our Western world. Belief in the goodness of creation has led us to explore our world in a scientific way. Belief in the goodness of man and the meaning of history has led us to organize life around "this life" in a way that many cultures have not.

Now we can understand what it is to say that Genesis 1 is a faith statement. We know what it means to say: "In the beginning God created the heaven and the earth." But what about all the other statements we find here? What about the order of creation and the seven days?

These, too, are faith statements, and we could examine each of the days to see why it is said in this way. For example, light and darkness are not so much physical terms as theological terms. Light is the opportune time for work; dark is a poor time for work. To say that God created first the light and the darkness does say that God created light as we know it, but it also says that God created the very opportunity for life and creation and *also the opposition* to life and creation. At the time

Genesis was written, *ca.* 500 B.C., it would have been clearly understood in the Near East that light and darkness are the two great original powers of the universe. The Hebrew people said that God created them.

In Babylon, astrologers said that men were determined by the sun, the moon, and the planets. The Hebrew people knew about this point of view, but they contended that God made these luminaries for the benefit of man. They had no idea that centuries later persons would ask if the Hebrew statements about creation were scientifically accurate!

Many Near Eastern cultures celebrated a "New Year's Day" by telling their creation myth and then dramatizing the victory of their god over death, chaos, or what have you. The Hebrew people did not have an identical ceremony, but they did celebrate God's covenant with man and especially with the Hebrew people. Genesis 1 – 11 was read at that festival; you will note the prominent place given to the flood and the promise given to Noah that henceforth the seasons would come in order so that man could depend on God.

The festival probably lasted seven days. It seems to me that the seven days mentioned here in Genesis 1 match the seven-day affirmation of God's love for and covenant with man. The last day does not end. This means that, in God's covenant, life is a life in God's rest — in fellowship with him such as Adam (mankind) had in the Garden.

In God's image

MICROVIEW 1b
Genesis 1:26-31; 2:18-23

In Genesis 2:18-23 we have one of the strangest popularity contests ever held. God lines up all the animals and asks Adam to pick out the one he would like most for a companion. As the elephant, the lion, and even the dog trot by, both Adam and God realize that an animal will never serve as the life companion of man. Man must live in companionship with someone like himself. Why is this true? What is man that he is different from Fido? These questions are answered by Genesis 1 and 2, especially in the "image of God" passage of Genesis 1:26-31.

In these verses it is said that man was made in the image of God. At first glance this would appear to mean that God and man look alike: that God has a head, arms, and legs just as we do. This is a very common conception of God in many cultures. We call it an anthropomorphic view of God (*anthropos* means man and *morphos* means form — hence "formed like man").

It is doubtful that the Hebrew people understood *image* in this way. The Hebrew people did not often describe a person or a building or even scenery. We have little idea about the appearance of Moses or David (except that he was handsome) or even Jesus, for the Hebrew did not distinguish between body and soul.

Our Western culture frequently thinks of man as a three-part unit which could be divided into its component parts if need be: body, mind, and soul.

But the Hebrew did not make this distinction. He could speak of person and flesh or body, but these are so related that they dare not be isolated. We are not souls that live in bodies, but we are persons that are known to each other by means of bodies. Put in another way, the person is "I" while the body is "me," that is, the person is my self as I know it and the body is my self as others know it.

Thus the Hebrews often used physical characteristics to describe the personality of persons. For example, *aph*, the Hebrew word for nose, also refers to anger. Evidently the Hebrews noticed that there was some connection between anger and dilation of the nose. This is really no different from our use of the word *sorehead*, which means one whose anger is easily aroused. We certainly don't mean the term literally!

In like manner, the mouth suggests or stands for commandments, the ears for obedience, the heart for will, the arms for strength, the bowels for compassion.

Eyes are important because they are the windows of the person (Ecclesiastes 12:3). In a person's eyes you may see all of him. When Genesis 29:17 says that "Leah's eyes were weak," it probably isn't referring to her eyesight. I think it means that Jacob didn't care for her personality.

Now it should be clear that the Old Testament probably does not describe God's physical image, but rather describes his person. If this is true, then the phrase "image of God" does not mean that we look like God, but rather that both we and God are personal. Later we shall explore further what this means.

How are we different from animals?

Another way to understand this phrase "image of God" is to ask the simple question, "How does man differ from animals?" If we know, goes the reasoning, we shall know how it is that God and man are alike. Historically there have been several answers to this question.

1. *Reason.* The most frequent answer has been that man can reason while Fido cannot. We can think abstractly about art, music, philosophy, and the like. Or we can proceed from given data to draw conclusions about an experiment. The lower animals cannot do these things; so we are tempted to conclude that man and God are alike in that they can use reason. One problem with this answer is that often, especially during wars and conflicts, men seem more irrational than animals ever are!

2. *Self-consciousness.* Another frequent answer is that man is aware of himself, of who he is and where he is, of his duty and his purpose. Fido simply responds to various stimuli without any awareness of his being a dog. He could not think of himself as a dog in comparison to man. Think of asking a dog to be a dog!

3. *Communication.* In recent years some have maintained that man is man because he can communicate. While modern man may be learning to tell bees where nectar can be found or speak with porpoises, it must be agreed that animal communication is very limited. It is a mark of man that he can express himself in many ways to convey feelings and ideas.

It seems to me that all this discussion about the "image" points to man as *person* and that the real point of this important passage is the *nature* of personhood. What is it to be a person?

First we note the interesting fact that in this passage God speaks of himself in the plural. The very word for God (*Elohim*) *is* plural in the Hebrew, but we do not often have plural verbs used with it. This leads us to believe that it has some special meaning here. Despite their affirmation of the oneness of God (Deuteronomy 6:4) the Hebrew people understood God in a plural way. They were able to understand a unity between one and several that persons today find hard to grasp.

We might illustrate the problem by diagramming several ways of relating the one and the many. One way is to conceive, say, of a chair which is perfect and real. All other chairs are copies of this one

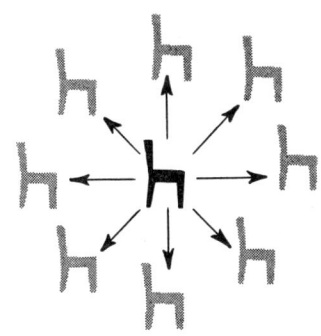

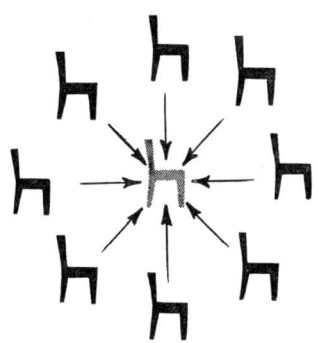

chair, the real chair which exists in the realm of the ideal.

Another way is to say merely that many chairs exist, and that our concept of

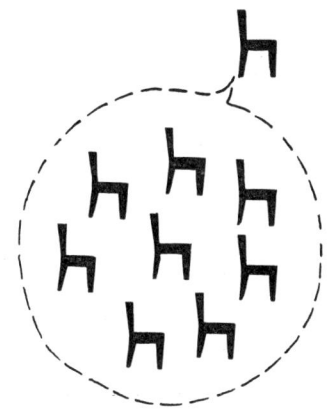

chair is simply a mental image of the many chairs we have seen.

The Hebrew says that all chairs are one chair. When you sit on one chair you sit on all chairs. There is only one chair and every chair is that one chair.

25

Likewise the Hebrew did not think of God as one ideal being somewhere up in heaven, nor as a number of gods running around. Rather, God is a unity of various aspects or persons, if you like. God is known to us through his Spirit. The Spirit of God is completely God, and all of God, but there is more of God! The same could be said of God's name, his glory, and finally his Son.

"Let us make man . . . many in one"

It is this many-in-one aspect of God which is underlined by the use of "our image." God is saying, "Let us make man as we are: many in one." And so man is made a unity. The human side of this unity is defined by the clause, "Male and female he created them." God made man like himself: a corporate being that finds his wholeness not in himself but with others, particularly with his companion of the opposite sex. At the same time man participates in the unity of God so that man likewise must find himself in relationship to God.

We might compare man to an oxygen atom, which has a valence of two, that is, requires two atoms of hydrogen, for example, to make a stable compound like water. Man also has an inner push toward unity and stability in his relationships with God and man. Every person must work out these relationships if he is to find fulfillment as a person.

This point is made by the "rib story" in Genesis 2. Man is a unit called Adam (mankind) and God divides Adam into two elements which are intimately related to one another (the rib is the bone closest to the heart). No person is whole until he finds himself in relation to another; hence the Bible says a man cleaves to his wife and they become one flesh.

It is important that we recognize the unity of the man-woman relationship with the man-God relationship. These two relationships are not identical (as many religions teach), but they are interrelated.

The Bible says many times that a break with man is a break with God or that a break with God is a break with man (Genesis 3; Psalm 51:4; 1 John 4:20). And just as the oxygen atom is unstable until it unites with another element, so every man feels at odds with himself when he is not in relationship with God and man. He is ashamed (Genesis 3:7), which means he lives with guilt, fear, and tension. Even if man seeks to ignore God he *knows* that in himself he is not a whole person; he needs fulfillment in a relationship. Every human knows that he finds completion only in another person. The need for the sexual relationship serves as a warning to him that he dare not "go it alone," and also serves the divine function of drawing him into a human relationship in which he comes to know himself in and through another person.

Worship and wholeness of family are key concerns

Appreciation of this fact helps us to understand the greatness of Hebrew faith. Worship is not just something that the community ought to do out of respect for God. Nor is the sexual relationship just a natural function in order to propagate the race. These two relationships are the very essence of life itself, without which one cannot enjoy true and whole life. This is why worship of God and wholeness of family are key concerns of the Hebrew faith.

The inner dynamic of worship and family are also interrelated. The Hebrew faith takes the point of view that the husband is responsible for the family in relation to God. Unlike other Near Eastern religions, the Hebrew faith has no wife for God; that is, there is no goddess. Man's relationship to God is a man-to-man dynamic. In like manner, person-to-person relationship is a male-to-female dynamic. Men are not free to know each other and women are not free to know each other until the man-woman relationship is fulfilled. These dynamics depend on each other, so that a man could not come to God without the relationship of his wife.

The great passages of marriage symbolism in the Bible must be understood with this in mind (Hosea 1-3; Ephesians 5:21-33). It would appear that the Bible is patriarchal (father-centered), but much that appears to be patriarchal is simply preservation of the inner dynamics between God, man, and woman without making sex and religion identical!

The Bible is quite frank here and when it uses the words "to know" it means the sexual act quite specifically. There were not many unmarried persons in the Hebrew community. We are not so fortunate today. The Christian church recognizes the need for these two relationships but says that for some it is a sexual orientation to the opposite sex without marriage itself (Matthew 12:46-50, 19:10; 1 Corinthians 7:38). In such a case the church serves as the family.

In summary, the "image of God" is a basic concept in understanding ourselves as persons who must live in communion. It will occur again and again as a guideline in studying the rest of the Bible.

The pair under the tree

MICROVIEW 1c
Genesis 3:1-11

A Jewish doctor once said, "You Christians think that sin came into the world because of an apple in the tree, but actually it was the pair under the tree."

He was right. We often place the blame for evil on someone else or something else or on creation itself. But Genesis very clearly says the problem was caused by Adam and Eve, every man and every woman.

In order to understand this, we must look closely at the condition of man as he comes into the world. Man is created good and the creation in which he is placed is good. There is no evil in it, nor in man. There is no devil or Satan that causes us to go astray. Instead, we are placed in a situation where we may have full life (communion with God and man forever).

Genesis speaks of this condition as the Garden of Eden. The Garden is anywhere life is found, from where the rivers of all life flow (the four rivers of 2:10-14). The Garden is real: it is the source of history and it is the condition into which each of us is born. Though it is real it is not a place to which we may travel; it is a condition of life which we have left and to which we may not return (3:24).

In this Garden there is a tree of life. The tree stands for the fullness of life which we studied previously. It is this life that God intended for us. It is this life that we all seek. It is this life which inspires our highest hopes, ideals, and visions. It is ours forever.

But there is a second tree: the tree of the knowledge

of good and evil. The presence of this tree spoils the whole thing. With it God lays down the law: If we eat of it we will die. This certainly seems like a dirty trick. If God intends for us to live in perfect communion, and if, indeed, this is the way we are born into the world, then why introduce the possibility of losing the whole thing? Why the second tree? This is a crucial question for understanding ourselves and Genesis 3. Let me give you an analogy.

Jimmy and the vase

Suppose I have a small son named Jimmy. Suppose I own a vase which I treasure very much. I would like to enjoy the beauty of the vase along with my friends and Jimmy, too. In order to do this I might handle Jimmy and the vase in several ways:

1. I could place the vase on a stand in my front room. In order to protect the vase I could tie Jimmy hand and foot, place him near the vase and say, "Jimmy, have a good time."
2. I could refuse to risk the vase and put it in one room and then take Jimmy to another room which is completely lacking in breakable items. I could lock Jimmy in the second room and say, "You are completely free here, Jimmy. Have a good time."
3. I could place both Jimmy and the vase in the room without any mention of the value of the vase or any command not to break it. Jimmy might never touch the vase and even if he did he would not be aware of the fact that he did something displeasing to his father.
4. I could place both the vase and Jimmy in the

room and explain very carefully to him the value of the vase. I could then say, "Jimmy, you are free to have a good time, but if you break the vase you will be punished."

Few of us would like the first example. It would be cruel to make of your son a slave who is forced to do your bidding.

Many of us would like the sound of number two. Most of us think it would be great to live without any rules, regulations, or laws. We think of this as freedom, but actually it is not. There is no freedom without choice and there is no choice without law.

The first two solutions are nearly the same — they both prevent Jimmy from exercising freedom.

The third example seems to solve this aspect. The vase is there for everyone to enjoy and, if Jimmy breaks it, he is unaware of guilt. But again this is another form of slavery. Even if Jimmy has possibilities of choice, there is not freedom until he *knows* there is a choice.

Only the fourth example will suit. Choice is given Jimmy; its terms are made explicit; he is trusted to make the proper choice; he is given the responsibility of making the correct choice; and he is informed of the consequences of his actions.

Man is created free

God does not want communion with someone bound to him; the relationship between man and God must be free and voluntary. In order to make man free and responsible, God must place in the Garden the second tree. God did not want man to sin, but he made it possible for man to do so by creating him free.

God's gift of freedom sets the stage for man's trouble

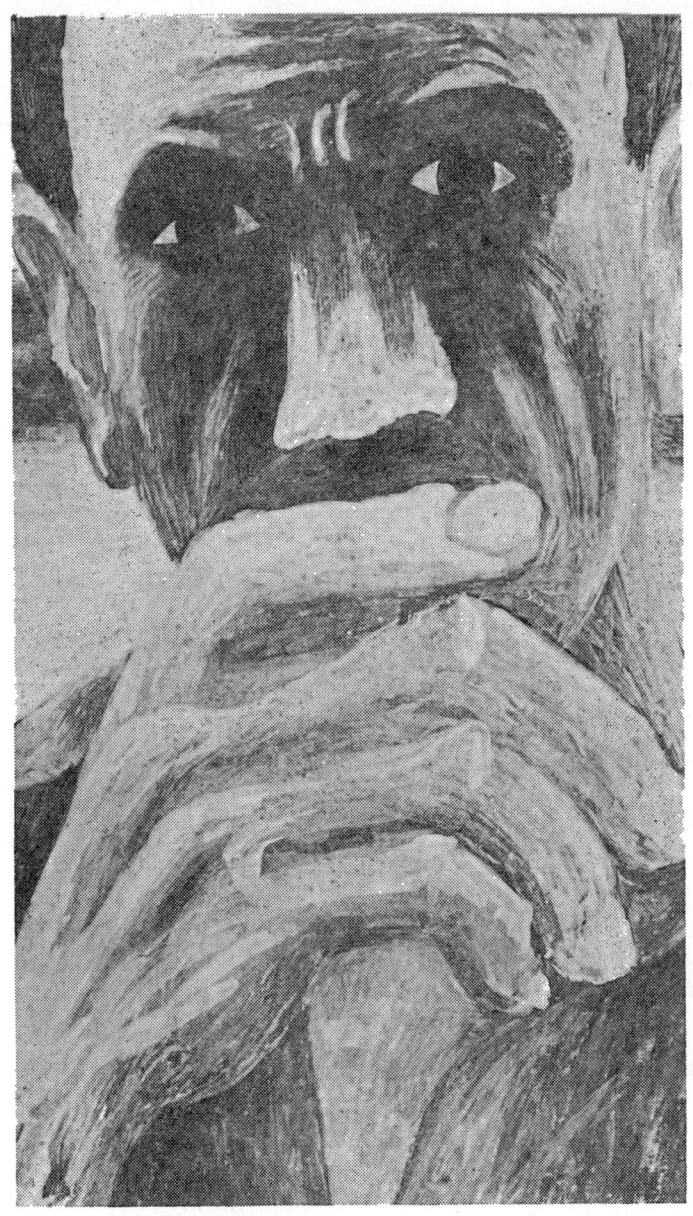

MAN by Ben Shahn, Collection, Museum of Modern Art, New York
Gift of Mr. and Mrs. E. Powis Jones

in Genesis 3. The serpent comes to Eve and asks her about the trees. There is nothing wrong with this conversation. If you expected some spectacular sin here you will probably be disappointed. The serpent merely asks what the rules are and then insinuates that the rules may not be for the best welfare of Eve.

We do not know why the figure of the serpent is used here. We do know that the serpent represents subtlety (3:1) and that this temptation was subtle. All that happens is the raising of doubt in the mind of Eve. Was it for our benefit that God ordered us not to eat of the tree of the knowledge of good and evil? Or is God withholding something really good from us? Doubt breaks the relationship between Eve and God; it creates distrust, and faith does not exist with distrust. This is what Genesis means by sin. *Sin is the small, subtle distrust which comes to exist between two persons or between us and God.* This small distrust results in attitudes and behavior we call "sins," but it is the break of faith which is *the* sin and which results in an action.

Eve tastes of the forbidden fruit and entices her husband Adam to do the same. As soon as they have eaten they know that the perfect communion they had with each other and with God has been destroyed. They seek to clothe themselves and to hide from God.

What is this tree of the knowledge of good and evil? We know that the phrase, "knowledge of good and evil," is often another way of saying "mature" (Isaiah 7:15f.). We also know that knowledge of good and evil is something God has (3:5, 22).

I think that Genesis 3 is a description of "growing up." The Garden is childhood where both trees are present but the tree of the knowledge of good and evil is not especially tempting. As children come to adolescence they are tempted to make life center on themselves and as a result create distrust among their friends, in their family, and ultimately with God.

Eve is tempted first because the girl matures sooner than the fellow. The sin is not in wishing to "know good and evil" or even in having "knowledge of good and evil," but in creating distrust by using persons for our own satisfaction. *Every one of us will do this. It is not necessary, but we will. Presumably we could attain maturity without creating distrust, but as a matter of fact we do not.*

What are the results of this "fall," this distrust which we create? According to Genesis the result is brokenness — alienation not only from each other and God, but also from life itself.

A basic function of woman, the conception and rearing of a family, becomes a painful process (3:16) as a result of the "fall." Henceforth children will be born in distrust and raised with alienation hanging over them as a fate, vividly illustrated by the story of Cain in chapter 4.

In Hebrew society the basic function of the husband was to protect and find security for the family. As a result of the "fall," man's relationship with creation is broken and in this brokenness nature fails to function as God had intended (3:17). Man toils hard, but receives thistles where before there were fruit and vegetables.

Finally God decrees that life is no longer "forever" but shall be limited. This is mercy rather than punishment. Life in brokenness will lead to chaos, as the rest of Genesis 1 — 11 indicates. God limits our span of life so that our lives and our history will not destroy us.

2
A wandering Aramean

OVERVIEW 2

Genesis 12 — 36

With Genesis 12 we enter the realm of specific history. Genesis 1 — 11 describes in the form of a historical story the condition of man and of the world in which he lives. God has agreed not to destroy the world but to work with man until the communion between man and God and between man and man is complete.

What follows is the history of an association of twelve Semitic tribes called the Hebrews, to whom God revealed his purpose and also the nature of the communion he seeks. While Adam and Eve are you and I and every man and woman, Abraham, Isaac, and Jacob are specific persons or at least represent a specific group of people. Because this is true it is quite possible for us to find out what these people were like, where they came from and what happened to them. In other words, we may study about them not only from the Bible but also from other sources.

The Hebrews' confession of faith

In Deuteronomy 26:5-9 we have a short confession of faith about what God did for the Hebrew people. This statement is a basic outline of the material from Genesis 12 through the book of Joshua:

> A wandering Aramean was my father;
> And he went down into Egypt
> > and sojourned there,
> > few in number;
> And there he became a nation, great, mighty and
> > populous.
> And the Egyptians treated us harshly,
> > and afflicted us,
> > and laid upon us hard bondage.
> Then we cried to the LORD the God of our fathers,
> And the LORD heard our voice,
> > and saw our affliction,
> > our toil,
> > and our oppression;
> And the LORD brought us out of Egypt with a mighty
> > hand
> > and an outstretched arm,
> > with great terror,
> > with signs and wonder;
> And he brought us into this place
> > and gave us this land,
> > a land flowing with milk and honey.

The material in Genesis 12 — 36 explains the statement, "A wandering Aramean was my father." There are two sections or cycles: Abraham is the center of attention

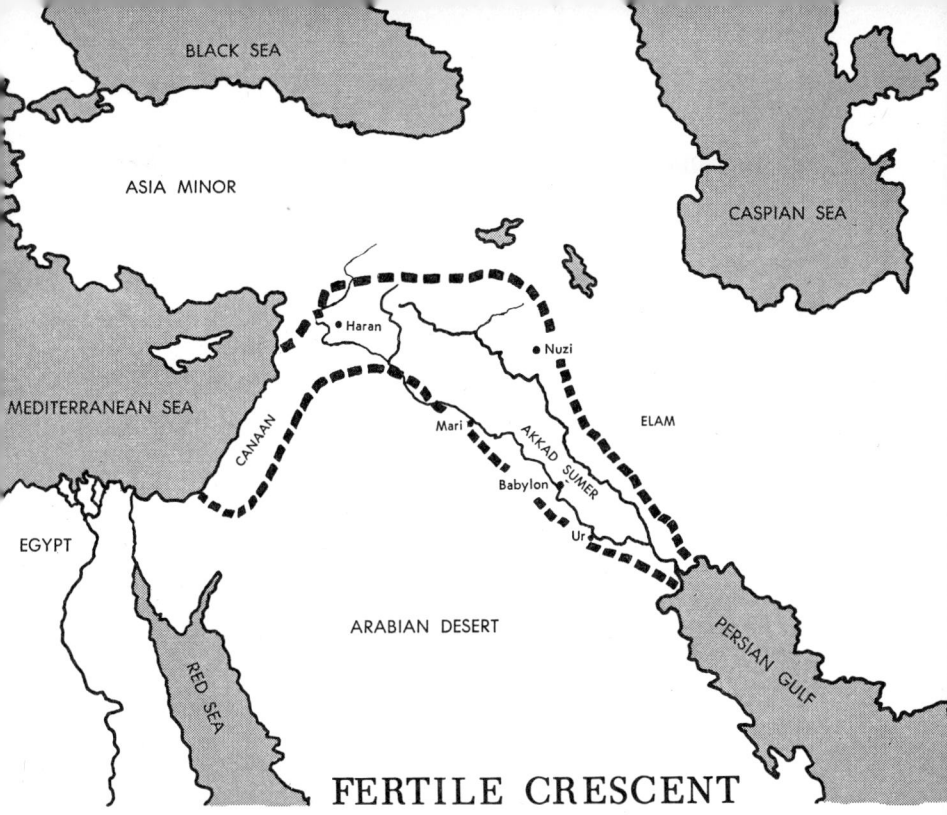

FERTILE CRESCENT

in the first (12:1 – 25:18) while in the other Jacob is the "hero" (25:19 – 36:43). But both cycles explain what it means to say that "my father was a wandering Aramean."

Who are the Arameans? To answer this we need to look at the ancient world between 3000 and 1500 B.C.

From the map you can see that the ancient Near East made a semicircle around the Arabian desert. The inhabited area moves north from the Persian Gulf through the Mesopotamian valley (*Mesopotamia* means "between two rivers" – the Euphrates and the Tigris) to what is now southern Turkey. At the foot of the mountains it turns south down the eastern end of the Mediterranean Sea through Syria and Lebanon to Palestine. *This semicircle often has been called the Fertile Crescent.*

Where civilization began

People have lived in the Fertile Crescent for centuries. Many historians consider it the cradle of civilization. The people living there were mostly farmers, with some businessmen. From this situation arose great nations and civilizations which were marvelous in what they accomplished. We know some of them: the Sumerians, the Babylonians, the Assyrians, and, just south of the Crescent, the Egyptians. These people developed very useful business procedures, had a high degree of scientific ability, and have left us buildings such as the pyramids which make modern man gasp with amazement.

But there were other people at that time who left us no heritage of business, art, buildings, science, and other products of civilization. These people lived in the desert itself or on the edge of the desert. For the most part they raised flocks of sheep and goats (or cattle in some circumstances).

At times, when desert living was too difficult, they came to the edge of the desert and either raided the farmers (Judges 6:1-6) or more peaceably served the villages as blacksmiths, soldiers, household servants, and workers in related menial tasks. Occasionally the desert people (nomads) were so numerous and powerful that they eventually took over the civilizations which they attacked.

Sometime before the year 2000 B.C. a large group of Amurru (Westerners) poured into the Fertile Crescent and were able to take over some of the states, especially on the Mediterranean coast. These people are known in the Bible as Amorites. A portion of the Amorites were known as Arameans, a group able to invade the northern part of Palestine and Syria with some success.

From various tablets discovered by archeologists we

know much about the Amorites and their customs. Many of their names and customs are identical to those found in Genesis. In fact, a class of the Amorites are also called the *Habiru.* This group seems to be a servant class within the Amorites. We suspect that these Habiru are the ancestors of the Hebrew people though it is not likely that all of the Habiru are identical with the group we know as the Hebrews. In any case we do feel confident that the Hebrew people were a part of the Amorite invasion, that they were a nomadic group seeking a portion of the Fertile Crescent. The part they eventually won was Palestine (see map 2).

The stories we find in Genesis are genuine stories about this period when the Hebrews or Arameans were seeking a foothold in Palestine. They are stories saved by the various tribes. The story about Shechem was likely saved by Simeon to explain why that tribe failed to gain a place in the North (Genesis 34). When the tribes were finally organized, the various stories from the several tribes were combined to form a single tradition about "the wandering Aramean."

While the stories used are historical, neither the order nor the intent of Genesis 12 — 36 is historical in nature. Again we should not be surprised to find varying accounts, say, of the birth of Isaac, or a confusing order to the narratives. We must remember that the purpose of the accounts is to stress the nature of faith and the mysterious working of God among men. Historical accuracy has little to do with this purpose.

As we look at Abraham, two stories stand out, one showing how difficult faith becomes, Genesis 21:1-21, and the other how Abraham became our "father in faith," Genesis 22:1-19.

Courtesy of the Oriental Institute, University of Chicago

A wall painting from an Egyptian tomb depicts family of

My father was a hobo

MICROVIEW 2a
Genesis 21:1-21

Members of *The West Side Story* gang use their parents as an excuse for the trouble in which they find themselves. Their parents were all fouled up; so why

Asiatics entering Egypt, perhaps during time of Abraham

should we expect them not to be? After all, this business of juvenile delinquency is simply a matter of complexes which need to be straightened out, they imply.

The Hebrew people also say that their parents were of little account. To say, "A wandering Aramean was my father," was not only a historical record, but a faith statement that their ancestry was nothing but a group of wandering nomads without a land, without any national structure, and without future possibilities.

Why stress such a statement? Would not the prosperous Jews of a later date be ashamed of their pitiful beginnings? No. This confession of faith says something about God, not something significant about the parents of the Hebrew people. God could have chosen some very fine people as his elect group:

> like the Egyptians, who perfected stone buildings, color paintings, powerful army equipment, and military strategy;
> like the Babylonians, who were great in literature and science and other areas of wisdom;
> or like the Greeks, who have been unsurpassed in philosophy and beauty.

In comparison, the wandering Arameans are a little band of tramps.

> How odd of God
> To choose the Jews.

How odd, indeed. With all the other great nations around, why the Jews? It is one of the cardinal points of the Bible that God does not choose people because of their value. Indeed, the Bible makes it clear that God does quite the opposite. He chooses those who are rejected, those who do not expect to be chosen, those considered worthless by the rest of the world.

Think how often he chooses the youngest son (Jacob, Joseph, David) when it is the oldest who is most important in Semitic society.

Think how often he chooses the country boy (Amos, Jeremiah, Jesus) to go to the city and tell the people there of his will.

Think how often he chooses the unsavory or uncouth character to be his servant (Jacob, Rahab).

Even the foreigner finds a major place (Ruth, Job).

God did not choose the Babylonians and the Egyptians precisely *because* they did seem the best. God chose the wandering Aramean so that the world would know that relationship with God is not something man can achieve but is something God gives. This reverses in a radical manner our way of thinking.

It is as if Harvard University announced that it will give a scholarship to someone without merit. Then Harvard searches throughout the United States for the most unqualified student it can find and gives it to him in order that the rest of us may know that this scholarship does not depend on merit.

So even the richest, even the most powerful, Jew must know that God's choice of the Hebrew people was not due to anything the Jews had or could do.

Faith is a gift

The stories of Abraham, Isaac, and Jacob dramatize this truth. Even though the stories are taken from tribal memories of the time when the Hebrew people were seeking a land, they are arranged to tell us that faith is something contrary to the way man looks at it and that even the fathers of "our faith" often lacked it. Faith was not something man could grasp; it was something given in life. With this in mind let us look at the story of Abraham, Sarah, and Hagar, with the two boys, Ishmael and Isaac.

In Genesis 12:1-3 Abraham was promised that he would have many descendants, that these descendants would receive a land and that they would be the means of bringing all men back into right relationship with God.

Several of the stories following Genesis 12:1-3 deal with the problem of Abraham's descendants. For example, Abraham and Sarah are forced to go into Egypt because of a famine in the Palestine area. Enroute Abraham decides that his life will be in danger because of the beauty of his wife. Since so much depends on Abraham (God's promises), he decides that he had best take steps to protect himself against the Egyptians. He proposes the rather unethical plan of passing Sarah off as his sister so that no one would kill him to get his wife. As a result Abraham does remain safe, but Sarah becomes a member of the harem of the Pharaoh.

By trying to protect himself in a compromising way, Abraham is in a bad position. He is safe, but the mother-to-be of the Hebrew people is about to become the wife of Pharaoh! Maybe God's chosen people will turn out to be Egyptians after all! But, before any damage is done, God makes known to Pharaoh the predicament and Pharaoh sends Abraham on his way. Abraham has some faith — he believes that God wants to use him. But he does not have the faith that God will see to it that his promise is fulfilled.

The problem with Hagar and Ishmael is similar. Abraham expects a son (15:4) after God promises him that he will not remain childless. But the time comes that he doubts that he can have a son. He is 86 years old (16:16) and Sarah is 77. So Abraham and Sarah have a family council. Their reasoning goes like this: Since there are not many years left in which to have a son and since we know it is God's will that we have a son, let us make plans to get one.

Now it has been the many archeological discoveries of the past few years that help us understand what happens next. According to the Mari and Nuzi tablets (records from the Amorite age), if a couple had no children it was quite legal for the wife to give her maid to the husband. Any child born of that union was the *legal*

Courtesy of the Oriental Institute, University of Chicago

Cuneiform tablet from ancient Nuzi containing list of personal names

child of the couple. In other words, the maid merely acted as a substitute for the wife.

The ways of God seem foolish

Abraham and Sarah adopt this plan of action to get a son. Sarah's maid, Hagar, is given to Abraham and after some time a son is born whom they name Ishmael. At first all is well, but in a few years the situation changes radically. God still intends that Abraham shall have a son of his own. When Abraham is 100 and Sarah is 90

God visits Abraham to make known this coming fulfillment of the promise (17:15-21). Abraham is so amused by the situation that he falls on his face and laughs. The ways of God do seem foolish to men who "know better." Sarah knows better, too, and she gets a real "kick" out of the whole thing.

Abraham is approached by three men while he is sitting before his tent at Mamre. After a meal prepared by Sarah the three engage Abraham in serious conversation. The point of the conversation is that Sarah will give birth to a son next spring (18:10). Sarah overhears the conversation and begins to giggle behind the tent door. It seems very amusing to her that the very God who made man and woman should be so ignorant of the "facts of life."

But the following spring she does have a son and she calls his name Isaac (because she had laughed — 21:6). And when Isaac is old enough to play with the other boys, Sarah cannot help thinking of the legal status of Ishmael — that he, not her own Isaac, is the true older son.

The day comes when she can stand it no longer. She orders Abraham to send the boy and his mother away. Consider, for a moment, how serious this step is. Ishmael is the legal heir; Isaac is not. It is wrong for Abraham to send his firstborn son away. Without giving them adequate food and water it would appear to be murder. Not only is it the wrong thing to do as far as human decency is concerned, but Ishmael has the emotional loyalty and love of his father. Abraham is displeased with Sarah's suggestion (v. 11). But in God's eyes Ishmael is merely the product of Abraham's impatience, while the son which God promised is Isaac. So despite the wrongness and the indecency of it, God tells Abraham to send Ishmael elsewhere and keep Isaac.

What was right and what was wrong? The question

is not answered by asking the world around us about what is legal or what is decent. Abraham was caught in a bad situation. The "right" was to do the will of God even if that meant going against his own desires and against the expectations of his community.

The problem is even deeper, however. Abraham and Sarah knew they were to have a son; so they produced one. But in due time God sent them a son. The agony of their decision with Ishmael resulted from their lack of faith and their reliance on their own resources to produce the will of God. The text tries to show us that God's will is not simply an objective "out there" toward which we may work. God's will is concrete but it must be accomplished by his means — through faith in him.

The father of faith

MICROVIEW 2b
Genesis 22:1-19

For several chapters the picture of Abraham and Sarah is a dim one.

Abraham endangered the promise of a son by allowing his wife to become a part of the harem of the Pharaoh.

He almost lost the promised land by allowing Lot to have first choice between the valley and the hill country (chapter 13).

He then took the situation into his own hands and produced a son by means of Sarah's maid. To his own chagrin, a real son was born to him and he needed to undo what had been accomplished.

Finally he tried to prevent God from judging the world about him by using the first countdown (18:22-33).

In all of these stories Abraham came off second best. How is it then that the Jews consider Abraham the father of faith? Why was it that Paul could write about Abraham as our spiritual father and not just the tribal father of the Jews?

The reason is captured in chapter 22. Here God threw out the ultimate challenge and Abraham responded.

Let us take a sharp look at what happened. The very first verse says that God wanted to test Abraham. Many readers, feeling that God would not test us like this, would remove this verse. In such a case the story is greatly changed; but first let us assume this is a test exactly as described in verse 1. In verse 2 Abraham was asked to take his real son, Isaac, go to the land of Moriah, and offer him as a burnt offering. Obviously nothing more difficult than this could have been asked, for Abraham loved his son very much, as does any normal father.

Of course such a request would be unthinkable today, but in Abraham's time it would not have been considered unreasonable. Human sacrifices occurred in Abraham's day, and evidently the Hebrews even practiced it occasionally later on (2 Kings 16:3; 17:17).

Actually there are at least two other reasons why this request of God's was profoundly difficult for Abraham to bear.

1. *Isaac was not simply the only son, but now, with Ishmael out of the picture, the older.*

In Semitic society the key to family and tribal structure was the oldest son. The oldest son represented the family when the father was absent (37:22). And, more important, the oldest son was the heir to the family fortune and recipient of the blessing.

The blessing, given to the oldest son at the time of the death of the father (chapter 27), carried with it the power of the family. The son who had the blessing would prosper, his business would grow, and he would have many sons. We today cannot readily understand this psychic gift. It would be as if a baseball player had passed on to his son his ability to hit home runs. Whatever the blessing was, the father lived on through the son who had it.

The ancient Hebrew people had no developed idea of the resurrected life as do we Christians. Consequently their "afterlife" was in their children, especially the oldest son. This is why it was so terrible a punishment to kill a man's sons before his eyes. It was not only the death of those whom he loved, but also the end of his and his family's future life (2 Kings 25:7).

Surely this termination of the blessing weighed heavily on Abraham as he responded to God's demand.

2. *God's command precipitated a theological crisis.* God had promised to Abraham that mankind would be redeemed through his "seed." His children would multiply and would be given a land and become the "blessing" for all nations.

As we have seen, Abraham had had a hard time accepting this promise for what it was worth. He had almost lost Sarah to the Pharaoh, he had almost lost Palestine to Lot, and he had become deeply involved in a vain attempt to get a son. But that was all behind him. Now he had a son — just one son. He and Sarah were old and would not have other children. If the promise of God to redeem all mankind were correct, then the fate of man, the very balance of life, hung on no other than Isaac. Here for a brief moment in history the redeeming plan of God hung on one person (as later it hung on Jesus).

Because of his previous lessons Abraham knew now what it is to have faith: to depend on and trust in God despite all human calculations and programs. But how could God now ask Abraham to destroy that very hope he had just given him? How could God ask Abraham to sacrifice the very one on whom the future hung? To ask him to destroy his own beloved son and his own destiny was difficult enough, but to ask him to destroy the destiny of mankind, the very purpose of God — that was too much!

These are the tests of Abraham. Few men, if any, have been tested to this extent: on the one hand his wishes, his future, and mankind's very redemption; on the other, God's stark command that he sacrifice Isaac.

Abraham responded by preparing for the journey. He took provisions, two helpers, and wood for the sacrifice.

There was no conversation. How could there be at a time like that? After a short trip the downcast Abraham lifted his eyes and recognized that he had reached the end of the fateful journey.

Leaving his helpers he went on alone with Isaac and the wood. Isaac asked the obvious human question: "Where is the sacrifice?" The answer of Abraham seems ambiguous, but it is the only answer which faith can give. He said, "I know it looks foolish to you, Isaac; and, since I know what God has asked, it appears even more foolish to me. I can only say that God is in charge and he will provide a solution."

The narrative goes all the way. Abraham bound Isaac, placed him on the altar, lifted his knife, and prepared for the fatal stroke. Abraham did not expect a miracle — he had passed the test. At the moment when it was certain that Abraham would give all, God stopped the process. As Abraham looked up he saw a ram caught in a thicket. It was the ram instead of Isaac that was sacrificed. God then expressed his pleasure in the faith of Abraham and repeated his promise of many descendants who would possess a land and become a blessing to all the nations (vv. 16-18).

The story of Abraham and Isaac is in many respects the key story of the Old Testament. Faith is the heart of the Bible and this story is the key definition of faith. The early church looked to Abraham as the "father of faith" (Romans 4; Hebrews 11). And when the crucifixion of Jesus became a powerful symbol in the Roman world, the Jews responded by stressing the near-sacrifice of Isaac as a symbol of faith and devotion to God.

It should be noted that many persons find it difficult to believe that God would test man this way. They prefer to ignore verse 1 and explain the narrative as the event which ended child sacrifice for the Hebrews. In this case Abraham simply does with Isaac what any normal father of that time would do — offer him as a sacrifice to his god. At the last moment God intervened and prevented Abraham from destroying the hope of mankind, Isaac.

From this point of view Abraham continued to misunderstand faith and would destroy real faith in the name of religious piousness. Such a conclusion is not out of step with the previous stories; and indeed the Old Testament frequently places faith over against religious practices and piousness (Psalm 51:16f.; Micah 6:6-8). But if the story of Abraham ends on this note, it would be hard to explain why the early church and the Jewish synagogue thought of Abraham as a man who really understood faith.

As it stands, Abraham did come to faith. His story ends with an amusing account of the purchase of a grave from the Hittites around Hebron (later the center of Judah). While the story exemplifies an ancient business transaction which still can be witnessed in the Near East, its importance is that Abraham and Sarah were buried in the promised land. Their graves stood as a sign that someday Abraham's seed would receive the land. In chapters 22 and 23 the promise of the Lord in 12:1-3 received a symbolic fulfillment.

3

He descended into Egypt

OVERVIEW 3
Genesis 37 — Exodus 11

The stories in Genesis 37 — 50 appear, at first glance, to continue the stories of Genesis 12 — 36. But a second glance convinces us otherwise. The story of Joseph is not a collection of narratives tied together by a theological lesson, but reads more like a short story with a definite plot. It has practically nothing of the action of God, no pronouncements of his promise, and only an external relationship to the theme of the Pentateuch; it serves to get the Hebrews into Egypt (45:6-8).

Otherwise the Joseph story reads like one of the many wisdom stories of the Near East. Its hero is persecuted unjustly (37:12-28; 39:19f.); he is capable of interpreting dreams; he can resist temptations (39:6-18); he gives counsel to kings (41:33-36); and he saves his people with his wisdom (45:7). Compare this with the similar story of Daniel!

These observations lead us to believe that the Joseph "cycle" was brought to its present form among the wise men or counselors of the court of David and used in the Pentateuch to illustrate the phrase of the confession, "He descended into Egypt."

The confessional story of the Hebrew people continues in Exodus, a book which, like Genesis, is composed of traditional stories from the three sources, J, E, and P, but is also united in such a way that separation into various traditions may destroy the intent of the total book.

The first part of Exodus is the story of Moses and his struggle with Pharaoh (1 – 15). It is climaxed by the miraculous deliverance at the Red Sea (chapter 14).

Once in the wilderness, the Hebrews learned what it meant to live in complete dependence on God (16 – 19) and finally were given a covenant with God their redeemer (20 – 40). The major parts of this covenant are the Ten Commandments (20:1-17), an explanation of the commandments which we call the covenant code (20:22 – 23:33), and ten commandments for religious observances (34:11-26).

The history of the period in Egypt is much more complex than even the story indicates. While with Abraham and Jacob we could identify some customs and movements which placed them in the Mari Age, *ca.* 1700 B.C., and made them a part of the Amorite invasion, now we are dealing with a specific country, a specific king, a specific "prime minister," a specific policy toward a foreign element, and finally a specific rebellion and successful flight.

Yet Egyptian court records take little notice of the events recorded in Genesis 37 – Exodus 14. This is not because their historical records are faulty. The Egyptians, like other Near Eastern peoples, kept quite thorough court records. We can find these today in the form of clay tablets and monuments.

Lack of such written evidence does not say that the events went unrecorded. It simply says that they were not of major importance to the court historian. But because there is little extrabiblical evidence of the Hebrews' stay in Egypt and because the biblical records themselves are very complicated by the intertwining of traditions, some persons are even willing to say that the exodus story didn't happen or at least that it is not important whether it happened or not.

The biblical writers had little concern for the part of Egyptian history that was involved. What did matter was that God delivered them from the hands of a powerful taskmaster and thereby fulfilled his promise to Abraham by creating a nation from nothing and giving to them a land of their own. Thus the Hebrews were not primarily trying to say something about the Egyptians and the Hebrews. *They believed that God was a God of deliverance and in pointing to the exodus story they were attempting to say something about the nature of God.*

Such a conclusion seems to be a radical solution, but it is a helpful one. It says that faith is not dependent on history. At the same time, faith has historical meanings; so it is written as history.

We could let the matter rest here, but many of us have just enough curiosity to ask: "When *did* these events happen?" In raising such a question we should not be concerned with proving or disproving the accuracy of the Bible or even with seeing what really happened. But such a question can help us understand the nature of faith and its relation to historical events.

Ramses II, who built several cities with slave labor, was probably the Pharaoh of oppression

Courtesy of the Oriental Institute, University of Chicago

We do know that the cities of Pithom and Rameses were built by slave labor. According to Exodus 1:11 these were the cities on which the Hebrews labored and the ones from which they fled. It is generally agreed that they were built during the period of 1300-1200 B.C. by the special effort of Pharaoh Ramses II.

Since the dating of the construction of these cities agrees with present dating of the conquest of Palestine, we can suppose that the Hebrews escaped from Egypt about 1220 B.C.

But Exodus 12:40 says that the Hebrews were in Egypt 430 years. This means that Jacob and his family would have gone down to Egypt about 1650 B.C. And, although this puts Abraham much earlier than the Mari period we have already used as his environment, many scholars have accepted 1650 B.C. as the date of the Hebrew descent into Egypt.

Another fact, however, complicates this seemingly simple solution. Moses was the great-grandson of Levi (Exodus 6:16-20) and unless there are gaps in this genealogy, 430 years seems an impossibly long time for four generations.

For this and other reasons, some scholars are coming to believe that the sojourn in Egypt was more nearly 150 years. Thus when all biblical and extrabiblical material is collected it seems most likely that the events in Genesis 37 — Exodus 14 occurred in the following period of time:

1370 B.C.   Joseph tribe descended into Egypt under Akhetaton

1360 B.C.   Other tribes went to Egypt during famine

1308 B.C.   Under Seti I the Hebrew people were forced into slave labor (Exodus 1:8)

Queen Nefert-iti was the wife of Akhetaton, who may have been Pharaoh when the Hebrews descended into Egypt

Courtesy of the Oriental Institute, University of Chicago

1290 B.C.	Ramses II came to power. Moses was born (Exodus 2:10)
1260 B.C.	Moses fled to Midian (Exodus 2:15)
1224 B.C.	Death of Ramses II, Pharaoh of the oppression (Exodus 2:23)
1223 B.C.	Exodus during Merneptah's reign (Exodus 14)
1200 B.C.	Conquest of central Palestine

If the above is true, why did the Bible report that the Hebrews were in Egypt 430 years? We could give three possible answers:

1. The authors did not know how long the Hebrews were in Egypt (if at all!) and used the figure 430 only as a symbolic "long time."

2. The time actually was 430 years.

3. The authors knew it was 150 years but said 430 for another reason. They only wanted to say that the entire period before the redemptive act of God was one of bondage. Accurate or not, the 430 years intended to include the period of the "wandering Arameans" in Palestine and not just the period in Egypt. Or, to put it another way, all bondage time is in Egypt (just as the modern American Negro may consider slavery "Egypt time"); so all time before the promise was fulfilled was *for the Hebrews* "Egypt time."

Odd as it sounds, I believe the latter answer is the correct understanding. We will see later that the same is true of the Passover, the giving of the law at Mount Sinai, and other major events in the life of Israel — similar

Courtesy of the Oriental Institute, University of Chicago

Canaanite captives in Egypt, from relief on temple of Ramses III

events are placed in their original context. All redemption is through the Red Sea; all law is given by Moses at Mount Sinai.

In this particular instance we have special help, however. As a matter of fact, the Greek translation of the Bible did understand the 430 years to be from Abraham to the exodus and it is this version which Paul uses in Galatians 3:17. Unfortunately we are not always blessed with such an early interpretation so that we can check our own understanding.

What does all this say? It is likely that we are dealing with some specific events in Egyptian history. There was a slave people; there was a Pharaoh that enslaved them; there was a series of plagues; there was a miraculous flight into the wilderness. *But the account we have is not a literal record of those events. It is a faith interpretation of them. What we have here is the faith granted by God to the Hebrew people by means of the events.* Event and faith are not identical, but event and faith are inseparable. Such an understanding of the biblical accounts will help us over many a problem yet to come.

Turning to specific passages we note that even though the Joseph story tells how the tribes went down into Egypt it still has an interesting point of its own in Genesis 44:14 — 45:3. In Exodus 3:1-22 we have the all-important revelation of Jahweh to Moses and to his chosen people even while they are in bondage.

A test of loyalty

MICROVIEW 3a
Genesis 44:14 — 45:3

As we have noticed, the "Joseph cycle" has a plot like a short story. Sometimes this is overlooked because we read the Bible by short sections and fail to see the overall picture. The climax of the story comes with the test in Genesis 44:14 — 45:3, but let us look at the total before we try to decipher the meaning of the "last chapter."

As you well know, Joseph was a favorite son but hardly would have won a popularity contest among his brothers. A part of the reason for their hatred of Joseph was no doubt the attitude of Jacob, their father. A good Hebrew father ought to be most fond of his oldest son, who would inherit the family fortune and blessing.

But the older sons of Jacob were children of Leah and her maid or the maid of Rachel (see chart). Jacob's real love was Rachel, and she had children only after the family was nearly complete. As a consequence Joseph and Benjamin were "darling babies" who received much affection from Jacob — to the chagrin of the jealous brothers. So the story of Joseph is in part the story of a family quarrel.

Joseph the dreamer

But Joseph was not simply a "favorite son." Joseph was a dreamer. We often think of the dream as idle night entertainment, but in the ancient Near East the dream was quite real and true to the situation of the dreamer. When Joseph dreamed he was the ruler, he really *was* the ruler! So even before he became the farm administrator in Egypt he acted as one to whom honor and obedience must be given. He had a ruling personality or soul. It was not an accident that later in life he did become such a ruler and that his brothers did bow down to him. Rather, this was what was to happen to him. He was a ruler even though he was only a youngster in the family of a nomadic tribe.

Such a view of dreams is not unlike our modern view in which the dream is also considered a part of our reality. But the modern view sees the dream as the release of suppressed thoughts while in the Bible it is understood as a means of communicating reality. Joseph could interpret these dreams because he was a man of God (Genesis 41:16); likewise Daniel was able to interpret dreams to the king of Babylon (Daniel 2:28). In prophetic

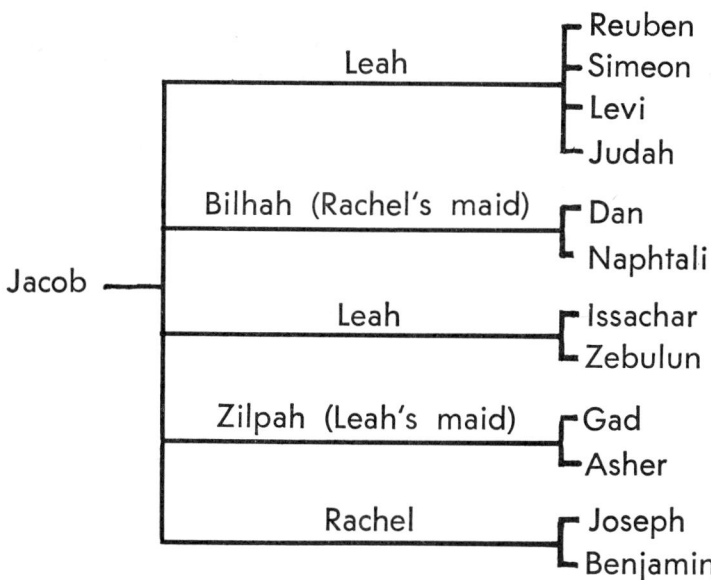

Jacob's Sons (in order of birth)

literature the dream was a means whereby God communicated to man (1 Samuel 3).

Little wonder then that the brothers of Joseph decided that they must get rid of this younger brother, who was not only the favorite of their father but also a dreamer of power. So they decided to kill him. But one brother was hesitant. Reuben, the oldest, realized that he was responsible to his father for Joseph and could not allow his brother to be killed.

The oldest was boss

In the family system of the Hebrew people, authority passed from the father to the oldest son and from the oldest son right on to the youngest. A group could not assemble without someone as a recognized and appropriate leader. Without such an understanding of authority and responsibility the brothers might have killed Joseph; but with it the group was more stable than we might have thought — considering the fact that the brothers strongly wanted to get rid of Joseph.

As a compromise, Joseph was sold into slavery and taken to Egypt. There God was with him and he rose to a high position in the estate of Potiphar (39:1-6). But the troubles of Joseph were not over. Potiphar's wife lay awake nights trying to figure out how to get the handsome Hebrew to sleep with her (v. 7). When he refused she managed to implicate him in a plot to seduce her, and Joseph was cast into prison.

Two points should be noticed here.

First, Joseph refused to sleep with Potiphar's wife because of his loyalty to his master and to God (v. 9). Joseph didn't say that sex is wrong or that he was morally pure and wished to remain so. *Joseph resisted this temptation because he did not want to break faith with his master and with God.* The Bible consistently places the ethical decision in the context of the trustful relationship and not in an outside law or convention or custom.

No reward for goodness

Second, despite the fact that God was with Joseph, Joseph was not rewarded for his evasion of temptation. Instead, he was cast into prison and except for his divine wisdom in interpreting dreams might very well have been hanged. *In the context of this world God does not guarantee health and safety as a reward for good conduct.*

In prison Joseph once again proved his mettle by interpreting dreams for his fellow inmates. His talent was later remembered and became the occasion for an audience with the Pharaoh himself. On this occasion he not only gave an excellent interpretation of the Pharaoh's dream (seven bumper crops and seven failures) but he also distinguished himself for the shrewd advice he gave about the problem. As a result Joseph was made second to the Pharaoh and placed in charge of grain storage and distribution.

When the famine years arrived, many people came to Joseph for grain. As the dispenser of life-giving food Joseph was a powerful man. Of course, the inevitable happened: the family of Jacob also was forced to seek grain from the Egyptian storehouses. As the ten brothers were ushered before the powerful official they were recognized by Joseph while failing to recognize him.

Joseph kept a straight face and proceeded to threaten them. He accused them of being spies. They insisted they were not, but were simply 12 brothers seeking food for their family. Where were the other two brothers? One was gone and the other was at home. Joseph insisted that they would have to bring the other brother to him to prove that they were not lying. He punctuated his demand by throwing them into prison for a few days.

Joseph overhears his brothers

After three days they came before him again. This time he said he would let them return to their father if they would leave one hostage for the youngest brother. At this point they spoke to one another in Hebrew and admitted that all this trouble had been caused by their mistreatment of Joseph. Little did they know it was their very brother Joseph who listened and understood perfectly well what was said.

They had passed test number one — they were sorry for their misdeed.

Joseph was so caught up that he nearly wept in front of them, but managed to keep up the false front. The bags were filled and their money was returned to them. Simeon remained in Egypt.

Upon returning home the sons of Jacob advised their father of the situation and insisted on returning for Simeon, taking Benjamin with them. But Jacob's sorrow over Joseph was too great to risk another "favorite son." He refused to let Benjamin go.

With the famine becoming more intense, however, it was clear that the brothers would have to return to Egypt. Finally Jacob was persuaded that there was no choice. He relented, but as a precaution he sent expensive gifts to Joseph as well as double the money found in the bags.

This time their treatment was vastly different. They were invited to be guests in the home of the mighty official! Furthermore, they discovered that the bags of grain from the last time had been paid for. At any rate, they were frightened by the invitation to eat with Joseph, for they suspected some plot. But there was none apparent. Simeon was restored; they were "cleaned up"; their animals were fed.

After all was prepared, Joseph entered. He asked of their father and then turned to Benjamin. Even the crafty Joseph nearly broke at the sight of his beloved full-brother. But after an interlude he managed to find control and ordered the meal to be served.

The brothers were amazed to discover the seating arrangement — in order of age! How did this Egyptian know their ages? But "darling" Benjamin spoiled the day again. He became the favorite of the official and received five times as much food as any other brother.

Kill the guilty one!

Now the stage was set for the final test. The happy brothers left Joseph and began the journey back. Joseph, however, had placed his silver cup in the bag of Benjamin. Then he sent his steward after the brothers to accuse them of theft. The sons of Jacob were embarrassed at first but reassured the steward that if they had been so honest as to return money from the last trip they would hardly steal a silver cup from their host. They were so sure of themselves that they told the steward to kill any brother who might have the cup.

One by one, from that of the oldest on down, the bags were searched. In the sack of the youngest, Benjamin, the steward found the stolen cup. The effect was catastrophic. The brothers had sworn safe conduct for Benjamin. Now they had invited the death of the very same beloved son by acting so proudly before the steward.

Coming back to Joseph, Judah pled for mercy. Joseph granted it except that the one in whose baggage the cup was found must stay. Joseph now had them where he wanted them. Benjamin was the favorite son, the brother of the hated Joseph. Now Benjamin was in dire trouble. The brothers needed no excuse to rid themselves of Benjamin. They had every legitimate right to leave Benjamin, the one apparently guilty of theft, with the Egyptian official, who, like their father, preferred Benjamin to them. Would they abandon Benjamin or would they remain loyal to Jacob?

Judah spoke for the brothers in what is one of the most moving speeches in the Bible. He stated again what had happened — that his father had had two sons by one wife late in his years; the two sons had been favorites and one was now dead. The other was Benjamin, the very brother accused of theft. If they did not return with him, Jacob would die of a broken heart. Out of loyalty to his father and his family Judah could not allow this to happen. Would the official please take him instead of Benjamin?

The brothers had passed the intricate test that Joseph had set up. They would not abandon Benjamin!

Joseph could not control himself any longer. He asked everyone but his brothers to leave and, bursting into tears, revealed his identity.

The rest of the story is anticlimactic. The sons of Israel returned to Jacob with the glad tidings. Jacob could hardly believe it all, but was convinced and eventually took the entire family into Egypt where the Hebrew tribes settled in the land of Goshen.

What's in a name?

MICROVIEW 3b
Exodus 3

The time came when Joseph died and Pharaohs came to power who had forgotten the important role played by Joseph in the crucial famine years. They could see only a foreign people living in one of Egypt's better areas. Eventually the Hebrews were made subservient to the Pharaohs and became, in essence, a slave state, used primarily for the purpose of building store cities.

As the lot of the Hebrews grew worse and worse, climaxed by an edict to kill all male infants (Exodus 1:22), God raised up a man to champion their cause. Moses was born of excellent Hebrew stock (the tribe of Levi), but was raised in the court of the Pharaoh. At an early age he recognized his identity with the enslaved Jews but in an ill-fated attempt to help them was forced to flee the country. He found refuge east of Egypt near the mountain called Sinai or Horeb. There Moses came to know a priest of the land of Midian (a Kenite) and eventually married his daughter Zipporah.

The cruel Pharaoh (probably Ramses II) died and was replaced by an even harder taskmaster (probably Merneptah). The time was ripe for the flight from Egypt. The stage for this action was set in chapter three of the book of Exodus. Moses was out on the mountain tending the flock of his father-in-law. There on the holy mountain Moses encountered a strange sight — a bush burning with a bright flame, but not being burned up. The strange sight was really a messenger (angel) from God, a manifestation which revealed his nature and purpose.

Courtesy of the Oriental Institute, University of Chicago

Scenes from daily life were recorded on the walls of an Egyptian official's tomb for his enjoyment in the next world. This painting shows slaves making bricks. Two slaves draw water from a pool. Others

And what did the angel or symbol say? First of all that God is a God of action. He is not a blob of pure stuff sitting around in heaven, but is involved in creating, in historical activity with persons, *e.g.*, with Abraham, Isaac, and Jacob. For this reason the manifestation here was a flame standing for aggressive action and movement.

At the same time God is not a chameleon. Though active and involved, he is not black one day and white the next. The God who made himself known to Moses on Sinai was the *same* God who was known to Abraham, Isaac, and Jacob. Therefore the bush was not consumed, that is, it did not change.

God then announced his intention. He planned at this time to fulfill his promise to Abraham by freeing the Hebrew people from the Egyptians and giving them a land flowing with milk and honey — Palestine. Furthermore, it was Moses who would act as God's agent.

work the moistened clay with small hoes. After the bricks are formed in wooden molds they are dried in the sun and carried to the construction site. The two men with sticks are Egyptian overseers

God gives advance notice

Here we learn another thing about God and his action among men. God announces his intentions beforehand. Biblical faith does not depend on the backward look. It is not a matter of interpreting events after they have happened, but the Hebrew knew ahead of time "what on earth God was doing." This is not to say that the Hebrew people always believed in what God was doing (as we shall see), but it does say that the biblical movement is always from a promise or an announcement to its fulfillment. Some man of God receives a vision of the coming events, or some wise man knows of God's purpose; then when the events happen they are understood.

The Hebrew was not surprised by history, for God is the creator and sustainer of life. God's people therefore know of what life must consist and the direction history will go. Such knowledge is powerful. It is the heart of the prophetic movement; it is the mystery which Daniel could transmit to the king (Daniel 2:28); it is the secret made known in Christ (Ephesians 1:9-10).

Moses could readily accept the action of God, but like many another prophet (Jeremiah 1:6) Moses doubted that he had what the situation needed. God insisted that the enterprise did not depend on Moses but upon his own action. At this point Moses pulled what to us is a surprise and perhaps even a ridiculous maneuver. He said, "No one will believe me. They will wonder who sent me. God, what's your name?"

To the Hebrew, and to those who think like the Hebrew, the name is most important for two reasons.

The name is powerful

Among many primitive people, to have the name is to possess power over the person. The name stands for the person and when you have that name you may control the individual involved. We know this mostly from voodoo, but actually we have many modern counterparts. Name-dropping is a modern form of getting power by use of names. Oftentimes to use his first name is a means of gaining power over a person. There can be little doubt that some power is involved in God's name. We have been taught to pray in Jesus' name because of its power.

The second reason is more likely the primary one, however. To know someone's name is to move from the realm of what we have called factual knowledge to knowledge in the relational sense. The name signifies the person and to know another's name is to enjoy a privileged or special relationship with him.

For example, we often use first names to signify a special relationship. Or if you live in a place where first names are always used you will likely devise nicknames or other diminutives to use with special people. Some languages even have a special form of *you* to be used with those who share first names.

When Moses asked for the name of God, he surely wanted power to act, but he also wanted to confirm a special relationship between him and his people on the one hand and God on the other.

The tradition we have called J believed that men had this special relationship back even before the flood (Genesis 4:26b). But the other two traditions (E and P, Genesis 6:2-4) maintain that only as the nation of Israel was formed at the exodus did men "know the name of God" — that is, have a special relationship with him.

Name-giving then has very important meanings. One cannot force God to give his name. Jacob tried that and failed (Genesis 32:29). God gives his name, his person, to those to whom he wishes to give it. This is what we call "election." God's people are called for a special job. As a consequence they enjoy a special relationship with God. Because the Hebrew people are elected to serve God in an extraordinary way, they receive his name. His name will dwell with them (Deuteronomy 12:5). One of the Ten Commandments is a prohibition against misuse of the name of God (Exodus 20:7) — a commandment broken many times by those who "drop the name of God."

Let us turn now to the name itself. What meaning does it have? God answered Moses with a somewhat peculiar answer: "I am who I am." The Hebrew words used here are the first person singular future of the verb *to be*. As you know, the verb *to be* has many uses in English. Very often it is a term of identity, *e.g.*, "This is a dog." It may also mean "existing" or "becoming," as in "I am on the way."

In the Hebrew language, when identity is meant no verb at all is used. But when becoming is meant, the verb *to be* may be used. This leaves a problem for the translator and explains why the margin of the Revised Standard Version of the Bible has also "I will be what I will be." "I am becoming who I am becoming" likewise is a possibility.

For many persons this revelation of the divine name defines God as "active being." Like the unconsuming fire, this name refers to God as true being yet always active and present. *God is both being and becoming.* It is something like a rosebud — all rose, yet becoming rose. Certainly the Greek translators thought of it this way when they translated it "I am being."

God went on to say to Moses that "Jahweh has sent you." The word *Jahweh* (LORD in the RSV) appears to be related to the word for *I am.* Many have taken it to be the third person singular of the same verb *to be,* meaning "he will be." We are no longer sure that this is true; nor are we even sure how the name should be pronounced, for the Jewish people of about the time of Christ held the name so sacred that they refused to pronounce it. Instead, they read aloud a word meaning master or lord. This is true in the synagogue to this day. We do know that when God revealed himself to Israel in a specific redemptive act he was known to Israel by a specific name with four consonants in it: *JHWH.*

Where the name came from is unknown. Many think Jahweh was worshiped earlier by the Kenites (represented by Moses's father-in-law). Mount Sinai was their "holy mountain" and it was under the influence of the Kenite tribe that the 12 tribes came to consider Mount Sinai their holy mountain and to worship God by the name of Jahweh.

Matson Photo Service

Jebel Musa, the mountain of Moses, is the traditional Mt. Sinai. Located in the granite mountains at the southern tip of the Sinai Peninsula, it has a rugged beauty and overlooks a broad plain where the Hebrews could have camped. Many scholars, however, dispute this location

Actually the origin is not very important. It is important that a special relationship between God and the Hebrew people was formed here. God is the father and Israel the son (Exodus 4:22) and names are exchanged. It is also important that in using this name the Hebrew people thought of God as active and powerful.

In fact, the name may have been more active than is indicated even in the text. It seems unlikely that such an ancient name as *Jahweh* could have such a calm philosophical meaning like *becoming*. It has been suggested that it was more likely a cry of exaltation during worship or other assemblies. In such a case the name is really two words which could be translated *Oh He!*

4

With a mighty hand

OVERVIEW 4
Exodus 12 — Numbers 36

The heart of the Christian faith is not in an idea about God, nor even an experience with God, but in an action by God — the resurrection of Jesus Christ. *We do not worship God because of custom or duty or logic, but because of our joyful appreciation for what he has done. He has saved us from bondage, bondage to things in our world which otherwise would destroy us.*

So also the heart of the Hebrew faith is not any lofty idea about God (like monotheism), but God's act of redemption (saving) at the exodus. Not only is it the central event of the Pentateuch, but it is the key point of Israel's confession and the cornerstone of its worship. In moments of trial or anguish, Israel always recalled God's special act of redemption:

> Restore us, O God of hosts;
>   let thy face shine, that we may be saved!
> Thou didst bring a vine out of Egypt;
>   thou didst drive out the nations and plant it.
> — *Psalm 80:7f.*

With the great importance of this section in mind, let us go back and review what happened. Moses returned to Egypt with Aaron and the two confronted Pharaoh with a demand to permit them to leave Egypt and celebrate a festival in the wilderness area. It was a reasonable request but Pharaoh turned it down. God and Moses countered with some plagues.

As the story continued, Pharaoh resisted more and more while the plagues mounted in terror until at the death of the Egyptian firstborn Pharaoh let them go. The Israelites moved toward the peninsula for their festival. Meanwhile Pharaoh changed his mind, and in the ensuing clash between God and Pharaoh, God conquered. The Israelites, now free, moved on (without adequate provisions) into the wilderness and eventually to Palestine.

Before taking Palestine they wandered in the wilderness without food and water, learning what it is to depend on God. At the Mount of Revelation, they received the formal covenant with God in the form of various commandments. Even while Moses was negotiating with God the people turned to idolatry and broke the covenant (Exodus 32). But the covenant was renewed and procedures for religious observances were set up (Exodus 33 – 40).

The story continues in the book of Numbers, which, like Genesis and Exodus, consists of the three strands of tradition (J, E, and P). The first part of Numbers (1:1 – 10:10) gives us a listing of the people at Mount Sinai, further religious and civil laws, and certain preparations for departure from Mount Sinai. In the second part (10:11 – 21:13) we have the journey from Mount Sinai to Kadesh-barnea, a journey fraught with complaints and rebellions on the part of the Hebrew people. The last section (21:14 – 36:13) describes the movement from Kadesh-barnea through the Transjordan to a spot opposite Jericho (see map 3).

A special part of this narrative is the story of Balak, king of Moab, and Balaam, a Babylonian diviner. Balak did not develop new weapons or techniques of warfare when the Hebrew army approached, but he spent his money on a great and famous diviner. War in those days was religious war, and the best a leader could do was invoke the gods against another army (2 Kings 3:27). In the case of Balak his plan backfired. In an amusing and fascinating story we are told that the greatest diviner of the East could only bless Israel because Jahweh was all-powerful.

Head of a Moabite king

Courtesy of Nelson Glueck

The story ends here as far as the Pentateuch is concerned. Leviticus continues with the regulations of religious practice. We shall consider this book briefly when we discuss the priestly movement after the exile.

Deuteronomy consists of various "sermons" by Moses. It is a book which very clearly adapts the narrative for a special place and time: the southern kingdom after the fall of Samaria, 722/21 B.C. Though it contains ancient material, we shall consider the book when we study Josiah. Now we might simply note that this adaptation is the fourth major tradition and we use the letter *D* to refer to it.

How Israel crossed the Jordan and took Palestine will be described in the next historical book, Joshua.

The careful reader of these narratives may note some difficulties in them as historical records. Again some reflection on this will often help us in understanding the nature of our faith.

A matter of numbers

For example, according to the census there were 603,550 able-bodied men above 20 years of age at Sinai (Numbers 1:46). Allowing a very minimal one wife and three children for each man (and according to Semitic customs that *is* minimal), we would have 2,500,000 Hebrews wandering through the desert area behind Moses, living off manna and quail. Such an army of people would have feared no one, yet they were frightened by Pharaoh's guard, by the inhabitants of Palestine, and by the kings of the Transjordan.

Or look at it another way: 603,550 men came from 70 men who entered with Joseph (Genesis 46:27). Such an increase in 150 years (or even 430) is a real population explosion! Before the modern population increase, Egypt itself was a country of only 3,000,000 people. How could such a large number of people become enslaved by a population of nearly equal size?

There are several ways to explain this large number of people. Some suggest that it is possible and that we are wrong in our data about populations. Others suspect an error in the text or transmission so that we have mistakenly come to the present number. I believe that the text is all right — that this is the number meant — but that this is a faith statement, not a historical record. There are several reasons why it would appear that this is not a single historical record.

1. According to letters received from Palestine and still recorded in Egypt there were Habiru in Palestine all the while that the 12 tribes were in Egypt. In fact, we have a stela (record in stone) of Merneptah which claims a total defeat of the Habiru shortly after the Hebrews left Egypt. We can understand this only if there were Hebrews other than those following Moses already living in Palestine! If this is true, not all the Hebrew people were in Egypt with Joseph.

2. As we shall see in the next chapter, it seems clear that after Joshua and his army crossed the Jordan they were joined by Hebrews already living in the land. If this is true we can say that a considerable number of the tribes were not in Egypt.

3. A check of all the place names in Exodus and Numbers indicates that nearly all the stories in the wilderness occurred at Kadesh-barnea, a well-known worship site for the Semites. The mountain visit is a pattern which has been combined with traditions of all the tribes (as we suggested in Genesis). If this is true it means that some of the Hebrews came to Palestine in a manner different from what we suppose in Numbers.

Courtesy of the Oriental Institute, University of Chicago

All of this leads us to one conclusion: There were some Hebrew people in Egypt, but not all of them. Why then does the Bible say all 12 tribes were there and why does it so specifically list the large number of families that took part in the exodus? As we have seen before (page 25), the Hebrew could think of one person representing all. It is crucial in this instance to recognize that what happened in the exodus has happened to all the Hebrew people. A Hebrew is redeemed precisely because "he was there."

Today, for example, even a person who becomes a naturalized citizen of the United States celebrates Independence Day. In a sense he declared his independence from his native country in becoming an American citizen. But the Fourth of July becomes significant for him and all native-born citizens because every American now shares in the freedom won by the 13 colonies.

I would say the same of the cross. All Christians share in the redemption of the cross. We all died and were raised. There were 900,000,000 people on that cross. I realize that this is not physically "scientific," but figuratively it is true.

I doubt that there were 2,500,000 Hebrews in Egypt physically, but figuratively it is very important that "all the Jews" were there. Even if Moses were the only one who was redeemed from bondage, it is necessary that the

The Merneptah stela has the earliest reference to Israel outside the Bible

presence of all is affirmed. According to the tradition that gives us Numbers, this population figure may have been the result of a census taken by David (2 Samuel 24) or at some other time during the monarchy period.

So we shouldn't scorn some of the details of Exodus and Numbers, but should continually ask: "What does it mean? What is being said to us?"

The crucial stories as they speak to us are first of all the meaning of the exodus itself and a description of the Passover event which even today is the Jewish celebration of the events described in Exodus. Chapters 12 — 14 contain this description. Much of Exodus and Numbers deals with the Hebrew people in the wilderness; so a second story of importance is a wilderness narrative, Exodus 16. And finally the nature of God's agreement with Israel is summed up in the Ten Commandments (the Decalogue) in Exodus 20:1-20.

God who acts

MICROVIEW 4a
Exodus 12 — 14

The story is told of a little boy who was asked about his morning's church school lesson. He replied that the Hebrew people were escaping from Egypt and that Pharaoh's army was close behind them in hot pursuit. Then the Hebrews came to the Red Sea and were trapped. Just then the American Fifth Army rushed in and built pontoon bridges across the sea. The Hebrew people crossed and, when the pursuing Egyptians were part of the way across, the Hebrews dynamited the bridge. The surprised father asked to hear the truth. The boy replied, "Dad, if I told you the truth you would never believe it!"

Unfortunately this is the normal attitude. We suppose that the action of God in the exodus is either supernatural (apart from our normal order of life) or else that the Hebrews thought it was supernatural but now *we* know better. Such a point of view robs the Bible of its basic message. God's actions are not "out of this world." They are very much a part of the situation in which we live.

If we witnessed or took part in one of "God's actions" we would likely think of it in political or sociological terms. But if we saw with "eyes of faith" we would understand these actions as God's work among men. *In other words, we should not consider God's action as something apart from life; nor should we dismiss his work as merely unusual natural happenings which a primitive people like the Hebrews would have thought were miraculous. If God is the creator and finisher of all things, then what happens in life is God's work and we should look at it in that way.*

Let's read the exodus story with eyes of faith! Moses goes to Pharaoh and engages him in a battle of nerves. Moses asks that the Hebrew people be released for a period of time so that they could celebrate their annual shepherd festival. Pharaoh refuses this request; so Moses and Aaron pull a few simple tricks to show Pharaoh their authority. These rod and snake tricks are, as we know from Egyptian pictures and records, stock in trade for wise men of the time.

Psychological warfare

When this ruse fails, Moses and Aaron use the flood of the Nile as psychological and theological warfare.

The plagues as described in chapters 7 — 10 are likely nothing more than a large flood accompanied by red clay (blood) and various bacilli which caused the diseases and led to dire consequences for the Egyptians, whose very lives depended on the Nile River.

The Egyptians believed that their gods controlled the river. The serious flood was a sign of their gods' disfavor and this was the lever Moses used against Pharaoh.

Actually the entire story is understood by the Hebrews as a battle between Jahweh and the gods of Egypt. *The struggle ends in a victory for Jahweh: the Egyptians lose their firstborn while Jahweh gains a firstborn (Israel).*

God takes the firstborn of Egypt (Exodus 12:23) as an appeasement, but he does not any longer take the firstborn of Israel *by sacrifice* (Exodus 13:15; see Exodus 22:29). Israel now becomes the firstborn of God (Exodus 4:22; 13:1f., 11f.). Israel becomes a living sacrifice — that is, one totally given to God but yet alive (Romans 12:1). This sacrifice ends in death when Israel, represented by Jesus, dies on the cross for all men (note in John 7:8 and 12:1 that Jesus deliberately waited until the Passover). This is the way that Israel understands what happened on that first Passover: they become the firstborn of God and death "skips over" them (the Hebrew for *Passover* means limp or jump, Exodus 12:13, 23, 27).

This understanding gets at the heart of the exodus event — an act in which the Hebrew people came into a "firstborn" relationship with Jahweh. But there is much more to the Passover than this. It might be compared to a modern Christmas celebration.

It would be interesting for you to check the origin of your family Christmas celebration. It is highly likely that your celebration is taken partly from your mother's family and partly from your father's family. And no doubt your grandparents had a mixture from their families. Your Christmas is likely the result of the mixing of many traditions — all adapted for 20th-century America.

Even the main elements of your Christmas do not go back to the first Christmas. Yes, the star, the manger scene, and the presents are original, but the tree and the candles were added by Martin Luther in the 16th century (according to some accounts). Americans have changed the candles to bulbs, and every country has added carols that would have been completely foreign to the angels on the first Christmas.

The way in which we worship does not often change very much, but it does change and develop according to the situation.

Hebrew worship is no different. The Passover has many elements in it. Not everything here is a part of the original Passover any more than your Christmas celebration is exactly like the first Christmas. But few of us wish to leave out the Christmas tree simply because there wasn't one in the stable that night. Worship material differs here from historical records. Worship deliberately grows and adapts to new circumstances; historical records do not necessarily.

There are three elements of the Passover: natural, historical, and religious. They belong together, but for the sake of understanding our religious observances let's examine them separately.

The natural elements

The natural elements connected with the Passover are really mixed up. The Near East has two seasons: dry from April to October and rainy the other half. The events of the exodus occurred in September and October. That was when the floods came and that was when the shepherd festival occurred. The shepherd festival was celebrated by the nomads to keep away the evil spirits ("destroyer" in Exodus 12:23) and to assure fertility of the sheep. A lamb was roasted like a shish kebab and served with desert plants (called bitter herbs).

Later on in Palestine when the fall shepherd festival had little meaning, this festival was attached to the spring celebration of the grain harvest. At the beginning of the (barley) harvest all old (leavened) bread was thrown away and a new start was made with unleavened bread. The harvest ended with the Feast of Weeks (we call it Pentecost). The Passover was then shifted to the spring and came on the 15th of the Hebrew month of Nisan.

Even though at the time of the exodus the Hebrew people were nomads or shepherds and would not have had a grain harvest, both the shepherd festival and the feast of unleavened bread are described in Exodus 12.

HEBREW CALENDAR

Hebrew Month	English Month
Nisan	March-April
Iyar	April-May
Sivan	May-June
Tammuz	June-July
Ab	July-August
Elul	August-September
Heshvan	September-October
Tishri	October-November
Kislev	November-December
Tebet	December-January
Shebat	January-February
Adar	February-March

PRINCIPAL JEWISH FESTIVALS

Hebrew Name	English Name	Hebrew Date
Rosh Hashanah	New Year	Tishri 1
Yom Kippur	Day of Atonement	Tishri 10
Sukkoth	Feast of Booths or Tabernacles	Begins Tishri 15-23
Hanukkah	Feast of Lights or Rededication	Begins Kislev 25 and continues seven days
Purim	Purim (see Esther 9)	Adar 14
Pesach	Passover or Feast of Unleavened Bread	Begins Nisan 15 and continues seven days
Shabuoth	Pentecost or Feast of Weeks	50th day after Pentecost

The point is that the Passover is a festival which celebrates an event in the natural season.

The historical elements

After the death of the Egyptian firstborn, Moses and the Hebrew people are allowed to leave. But once again Pharaoh changes his mind and sends border guards after a slow Hebrew caravan. Just as the tribes seem caught in a trap, they manage to elude the guards and escape into the desert of the Sinai peninsula. The J tradition makes the escape rather simple: the Hebrews did not sink in the mud while the Egyptian chariots did. If we assembled the J account it would go something like this:

When the king of Egypt was told that the people had fled, the mind of Pharaoh and his servants was changed toward the people, and they said, "What is this we have done, that we have let Israel go from serving us?" So he made ready his chariot and took his army with him, and took six hundred picked chariots and all the other chariots of Egypt with officers over all of them.

. . . The people of Israel lifted up their eyes, and behold, the Egyptians were marching after them; and they were in great fear . . .; and they said to Moses, "Is it because there are no graves in Egypt that you have taken us away to die in the wilderness? What have you done to us, in bringing us out of Egypt? Is not this what we said to you in Egypt, 'Let us alone and let us serve the Egyptians'? For it would have been better for us to serve the Egyptians than to die in the wilderness." And Moses said to the people, "Fear not, stand firm, and see the salvation of the Lord, which he will work for you today; for the Egyptians whom you see today, you shall never see again. The Lord will fight for you, and you have only to be still."

Then the angel of God who went before the host of Israel

moved and went behind them; and the pillar of cloud moved from before them and stood behind them, coming between the host of Egypt and the host of Israel. And there was the cloud and the darkness; and the night passed without one coming near the other all night.

And in the morning watch the LORD in the pillar of fire and of cloud looked down upon the host of the Egyptians, and discomfited the host of the Egyptians, clogging their chariot wheels so that they drove heavily; and the Egyptians said, "Let us flee from before Israel; for the LORD fights for them against the Egyptians." . . . And the sea returned to its wonted flow when the morning appeared; and the Egyptians fled into it, and the LORD routed the Egyptians in the midst of the sea.

Thus the LORD saved Israel that day from the hand of the Egyptians; and Israel saw the Egyptians dead upon the seashore. And Israel saw the great work which the LORD did against the Egyptians, and the people feared the LORD; and they believed in the LORD and in his servant Moses.

— *Exodus 14:5-7, 10bc, 11-14,*
19-20, 24-25, 27b, 30-31

The J account is concerned only that at this moment Israel became a nation by the mercy of God. The writer stresses the action of God in history and the Passover celebrates the event and keeps it in the memory of all later Hebrews.

The religious elements

Later accounts alter the picture. *By the time of the exile, 586-539* B.C., *the Passover had become the central symbol of God's redemption of man. Whenever redemption occurs it is "an exodus."* The symbol of this is passing through water — the water of the first chaos (Genesis 1:2) or the water of the Jordan (Joshua 4:23).

Note how Isaiah of Babylon can compare the return from exile to the redemption of creation as well as that of the exodus:

> Awake, awake, put on strength,
> > O arm of the LORD;
> awake, as in days of old,
> > the generations of long ago.
> Was it not thou that didst cut Rahab in pieces,
> > that didst pierce the dragon?
> Was it not thou that didst dry up the sea,
> > the waters of the great deep;
> that didst make the depths of the sea a way
> > for the redeemed to pass over?
> And the ransomed of the LORD shall return,
> > and come with singing to Zion;
> everlasting joy shall be upon their heads;
> > they shall obtain joy and gladness,
> > and sorrow and sighing shall flee away.
>
> > > — *Isaiah 51:9-11*

Or the psalmist compares the exodus to the crossing of the Jordan:

> The sea looked and fled,
> > Jordan turned back.
> The mountains skipped like rams,
> > the hills like lambs.
> What ails you, O sea, that you flee?
> > O Jordan, that you turn back?
> O mountains, that you skip like rams?
> > O hills, like lambs?
> Tremble, O earth, at the presence of the Lord,
> > at the presence of the God of Jacob,
> who turns the rock into a pool of water,
> > the flint into a spring of water.
>
> > > — *Psalm 114:3-8*

With this religious element becoming the main aspect of the Passover we are not surprised to see that the latest tradition, P, emphasizes the water of the Red Sea far beyond the other accounts. P has God blowing the water up like a wall so that the Israelites may walk through it and be saved. The water then closes over the Egyptians and destroys them. For Isaiah, the psalmist, and the priestly tradition, God has conquered the power of evil in the exodus; *by participating in the Passover meal the Jew shares in God's victory over evil.*

What are the Passover and the exodus? They are a seasonal time of renewal which corresponds to the time when Israel was redeemed from bondage and calls for Israel also to renew her faith in God's action among men.

Our daily bread

MICROVIEW 4b

Exodus 16

Food and drink! Bread and circuses! The everlasting problem of people living together is to keep them happy. From the Coliseum in ancient Rome to Capitol Hill in Washington the question has been "How do we keep them satisfied?"

The people of the Bible are no different. I know that we today have somehow gained the opposite opinion. We think the Old Testament people of God must have lived a very puritanical and severe life; we picture the early disciples as saints; and we think of copying the early church.

How remarkedly different is the actual picture! It never ceases to amaze me that the very chapter that follows the exodus narrative can describe the Hebrew people as a crew of complainers and malcontents. By a miraculous maneuver the pursuing Egyptian guard was thwarted and the mass of unarmed, ill-prepared Hebrew families was not only allowed to go into the wilderness but found themselves free to leave the land of bondage!

At first it went well with the "people of God." They were no doubt proud of their leader, Moses, and were eager to climb on the bandwagon of success. But they had come prepared for just a week-long festival, and after three days their water supply ran low. They finally came to a well called Marah, whose water, because of its bitterness, was impossible to drink. Disappointed and thirsty, the motley crowd began to grumble about their leadership. "What shall we drink?" they cried out. Moses and Jahweh were up to the situation and they managed to make the water fit to drink. In fact, God even promised to make them disease-free (Exodus 15:26).

Continuing on into the desert, they finally came to an oasis called Elim where at least their thirst was quite satisfied. On the other hand, they had been away from Egypt some 40 days and their last scrap of bread was gone. Their plight was not enviable. They were a large company of people, far from any source of food. How should they continue to survive? Moses had presented no plan. Up to this moment his platform had been a religious one and it included no planks on agriculture or food storage.

Being ordinary people and not a superrace, they began to think of all the things they had left behind. Back in Egypt they had sat beside the stew kettle and with all the bread they could use had dipped into the meat dish (Exodus 16:3). The hungrier they became the more they remembered each item on the Egyptian table. "O that we had meat to eat! We remember the fish we ate in Egypt for nothing, the cucumbers, the melons, the leeks, the onions, and the garlic" (Numbers 11:5).

Naturally Moses was upset by their lack of courage and faith. Their grumbling was not really against him, he insisted, but against the Lord, who had brought them to this place. And the Lord would provide. Jahweh had said he would rain bread from heaven. Every morning they could go out and take all they wanted for the day. Not only would they get bread, said Jahweh, but in the evening quail would come to them in sufficient numbers that they could have meat, too.

As long as the Hebrews were in the wilderness, this arrangement continued. The people then began to grumble at this steady diet. Once Jahweh was so angry about the complaints that he threatened to stuff meat down their throats until it came out of their noses (Numbers 11:20). We know what the food was. As Exodus 16:31 suggests, the manna was a seed or secretion from the coriander bush. And the quail still fly over the desert region of Mount Sinai. But this is not the point.

The newly formed "people of God" supposed that their life depended on their ability to achieve; but God sought to teach them otherwise. Time and time again this was the point of their life in the wilderness. They sought water, bread, and meat. God gave them all of these. They sought a religious experience and religious exercises (Exodus 32). God gave them his own glory. They sought more leaders and political power for themselves. God sent his spirit (Numbers 11). They sought to take the land of Canaan on their own but could not (Numbers 13, 14). God gave them the land.

Depending on God

Down through the centuries the experience of Israel in the wilderness has become a symbol of what it means to depend on God. In 750 B.C., Hosea views the wreck of what was once "God's people." Now they worship false gods. They are not true to each other for they take advantage of the weak among them. Love is gone. Hosea thinks back on the time when Israel and God first had a covenant. God says:

> Like grapes in the wilderness,
>   I found Israel.
> Like the first fruit on the fig tree,
>   in its first season.
> *—Hosea 9:10*

God remembers how he taught Israel (Ephraim) the basic

"facts of life" — in this case how to live by faith and dependence on God.

> When Israel was a child, I loved him,
>   and out of Egypt I called my son.
> Yet it was I who taught Ephraim to walk,
>   I took them up in my arms;
>   but they did not know that I healed them.
> I led them with cords of compassion,
>   with the bands of love,
> and I became to them as one
>   who eases the yoke on their jaws,
>   and I bent down to them and fed them.
>
> *— Hosea 11:1, 3f.*

Now the people are fat and prosperous. They disregard God. They offer him sacrifices as if that would make up for the hardness of their hearts and the wrongness of their ways. For Hosea there is only one way out — back to the wilderness. Israel once again must experience a period of dependence, of not knowing where the next meal will come from.

> Therefore, behold, I will allure her,
>   and bring her into the wilderness,
>   and speak tenderly to her.
> And there I will give her her vineyards,
>   and make the valley of Achor a door
>   of hope.
> And there she shall answer as in the days
>   of her youth,
>   as at the time when she came out of
>   the land of Egypt.
>
> *— Hosea 2:14-15*

In the New Testament we find an even deeper meaning for "bread" and the wilderness period. When Jesus taught us to pray, "Give us our daily bread," he meant that we should live in this type of dependence on God. The early church understood its own life as a sort of wilderness existence. In John 6, Jesus said it was true that the Jews received bread in the wilderness, but God would give them the true bread. The disciples wanted to know what this true bread was; and Jesus replied, "I am the bread of life."

The early church understood by this that those who participate in the "body" of Christ eat the true bread of life — they are the ones really living by faith in God. Consequently to take of the bread becomes a very important symbol of the church. It means that we understand that life comes from God and that by taking what he gives us we may have "real life."

Paul said (1 Corinthians 10:1-5) much the same when he compared baptism with a passing through the Red Sea and then claimed that the water which came from the rock was Christ (Exodus 17:1-6). *In other words, our life in the church is a wilderness life — a life in which we come to depend upon and have faith in God's leading and intent.* This life is not easy, as we see from the grumbling of the Jews; nor is it a lazy one. But it is life that satisfies. It is our daily bread.

Smoke on the mountain

MICROVIEW 4c
Exodus 20:1-20

The Hebrew people were led to Mount Sinai by a pillar of fire and a cloud. Now, as they came to the Mount of Revelation, God spoke from the smoke and gave basic guidance for all men.

As the people stood before Mount Sinai, God reminded them once again of what he had done for them (Exodus 19:4) and why he elected them. He chose them to be a kingdom of priests and a holy nation (Exodus 19:6). This responsibility did not mean that the people did not need priests and holy things. It meant instead that the Hebrew people would be the priests for all men; *the nation was set aside to bring God's will to all men and to intercede with God for all men.* Israel was set aside for this specific religious function (*holy* means set aside for a specific purpose).

But in the covenant relationship man also has a responsibility: *to keep the relationship whole and to witness to others about the nature of life with God. For this reason Israel had received from God the basic law of life: the Ten Commandments.*

When we use this word *law* for the Ten Commandments we need to understand what we mean. Some laws may be given simply to demonstrate the power of the ruler over others (dictatorship), but the laws of the Bible are not of that nature. God is no tyrant. Other laws are set up by society to protect people from one another; if you break one of these laws you are penalized in some way. While such laws are found in the Bible, they are what we call case laws or *casuistic* laws. They read, "If you do so and so, then so and so will be the penalty."

The Ten Commandments, however, are direct laws about the relationship of man with God and man with man; to break these laws does not mean that God and society will give you a trial and convict you. *To break these laws is to violate the primary relationship we noticed in Genesis; the result is alienation or brokenness.* The Ten Commandments are a basic statement about the nature of life in covenant with God. They are stated categorically: *Thou shalt.* We call this *apodictic* law.

So it is then that the first four of the commandments deal with our relationship to God; we call these the first tablet. The last six commandments deal with the human relationships; we call them the second tablet. Now let us look at the commandments individually.

1. *You shall have no other gods before me.*

This is not a plea for monotheism. Indeed, monotheism is no great theme of the Bible. One can easily worship one god which is the wrong god. According to our study in Genesis we remember that every person *must* relate in some way to God and man. Each of us has a god. In biblical terms these gods are very real to us and we may give our lives to them: family, car, money, prestige, sex, power. Such a god will destroy us for it is not the living God. It is essential that we not place a false god between us and the God of life.

2. *You shall not make for yourself a graven image.*

Many people make statues or figurines to stand for their god. They place these figurines in places of worship and worship their gods through the visible figures. The problem here is not so much that man therefore worships a false god, but that relational knowledge tends to be-

Courtesy of the Oriental Institute, University of Chicago

Hammurabi stands before the sun god Shamash, patron god of justice. Hammurabi's Code, recorded on the bottom portion of this stela, contains almost 300 case laws. In contrast, the Decalogue consists of apodictic laws, unique with Israel

come factual. God is reduced to an image that man can placate and influence and manipulate.

Often we use God as a tool for making ourselves or our nation psychologically healthy. God then is only a mechanism. So we still have the difficulty of reducing God to "facts" even though we do not always make a statue of the "facts" we have produced.

The graven image destroys man's vital relationship with God.

3. *You shall not take the name of the Lord your God in vain.*

As we have already seen, the name of God actually represents God. Moses needed the name of God before he could go to the Hebrew people. The name creates power. So we pray in the name of Jesus. Knowing the name of God also indicates the intimate relationship we call worship and communion.

Within this intimate relationship we may not use God or his power (name) to our own advantage and gratification, to be "holy name-droppers." We may not use our relationship with God to condemn others, to put others in their place, to add to our prestige, to insure our truthfulness and honesty, to gain special favors. Such action would be to take the name of God in vain — to use God for our advantage.

One may not remain faithful to God and use God at the same time.

4. *Remember the Sabbath day, to keep it holy.*

As we noticed in Genesis, the Sabbath was the time when God and man could together enjoy the creation. *Sabbath* stands for that rest and that fellowship which characterize the relationship between man and God. But man turned from God and left that fellowship.

In a world which is alienated from God, man must periodically set aside time for communion. This is the Sabbath. You would not think of marrying someone and then living in separate houses or even different towns. Yet many people claim to have a covenant with God and never live in the same house with him, or set aside specific times to be with him. Men like to think of God abstractly so that they can worship him abstractly (on the golf course).

The Ten Commandments put it otherwise: God is personal, and personal communion requires a time and a place.

These four commandments are essential to right relationships with God: no false gods, no depersonalization, no misuse of the relationship, and reservation of periodic times for communion.

Now what about the relationships between persons?

5. *Honor your father and your mother.*

At first glance this seems like a rather foolish commandment to head up a list of basic laws in human relationships. But a second look may make us think otherwise. If, as we have maintained, the family is central in Hebrew society and the man-woman relationship is the key human relationship, then, as trust in God is the basic divine command, so trust in family is the basic human command. Distrust of father and mother always results in social brokenness. This is a difficult commandment, because in human society parents sometimes are not worthy of our trust. But this commandment is not a blind law; it merely states the truth that distrust in the family breeds social distrust.

If we cannot trust our parents, for whatever reason, we must know that we will be deeply affected by this loss.

6. *You shall not kill.*

Properly speaking, this is a prohibition against murder. It does not speak specifically to the problem of warfare *within Hebrew society.*

It simply states the obvious truth: One cannot enjoy a covenant relationship with his fellowman and, at the same time, kill him.

7. *You shall not commit adultery.*

Adultery is a serious matter because it not only destroys the basic unit, the family, but it also destroys faith among men and women in the community. Even anthropologists (specialists in the study of man) have observed that community does not exist where adultery is permitted. Primitive tribes in which marriages may be polygamous (more than one wife) or polyandrous (more than one husband) have rules prohibiting adultery.

8. *You shall not steal.*

This commandment is equally clear. In Hebrew society, property is a part of the person. If an ox gores someone the owner is responsible. To take property from another is to destroy, in some sense, his person. To take to yourself another person's property likewise destroys you (guilt in our language). Such a situation destroys the covenant relationship.

9. *You shall not bear false witness.*

Justice in the Bible is the restoration of the broken relationship. Justice is not met when a fine has been paid or a sentence carried out. Justice is covenantal; it preserves the covenant. So when one man commits a crime against another, it is necessary that steps be taken to restore faith between these two covenant brothers.

This process is the Hebrew system of justice. Now

if someone witnesses in this process and does not tell the truth, then the relationship will never be restored. The men involved will come to the end of their lives in brokenness. According to Hebraic thinking, these men will know that something is wrong but, because of the false witnesses, will not be able to identify it.

So bearing false witness (perjury) prevents justice and becomes a serious block to the covenantal relationship.

10. *You shall not covet.*

Much of the second tablet can be identified in the outer act of man. Adultery, murder, theft, perjury, and even family unity can be observed by man and these actions can be handled by the laws of the community.

But man's relationship to man can be broken from within. If a man desires another man's house, or something else which he possesses, or if he wishes for his wife instead of his own, then *already* he has broken with his own family and begins to break with his neighbor. This is not a prohibition in the sense of a legal code, but a statement that if you wish to remain in covenant unity you must not covet. Compare this with the Sermon on the Mount:

"Every one who is angry with his brother shall be liable to judgment.

"Every one who looks at a woman lustfully has already committed adultery with her in his heart."

Faith in God is a relationship of trust. *Abraham learned that one cannot establish trust simply by following a program or some laws — no matter how good they may be!* Faith is not bound to any laws or morals; faith is not bound to any religious system or practice; faith is the relationship of trust, and *nothing* may define or limit faith.

It is good news (gospel) when we learn that God will grant to us the relationship of faith even though we have broken with him. We cannot earn this — God gives it to us.

Having said this, though, we now see that the faith relationship carries with it moral and religious implications. Just as eating of the tree of good and evil breaks our relationship with God in the Garden, so breaking the Ten Commandments automatically cancels our relationship of faith. *Law does not give us faith, but faith does not exist without law.*

5

A land flowing with milk and honey

OVERVIEW 5
Joshua, Judges

After living on manna and quail for several years, one would think, even the most meager of diets would taste like "milk and honey." Canaan (Palestine) was not exactly the garden spot of the world. It is not now and was not then.

All the phrase means is that the nomadic tribes became farmers. They gave up shepherding and settled down to a more stable life raising grapes and figs, grain and lentils along with the lucrative item — olives. In terms of our previous discussion, the taking of Canaan was nothing more than a common socio-economic movement — some wandering tribes cross the edge of the desert and try the more settled life for a while.

Both the Bible and archeological findings help us

Matson Photo Service

An aerial view of the Jordan north of where the Hebrews crossed into Canaan shows the stark contrast between the fertile and the arid areas of the land

understand how this movement happened. We said before that some of the Hebrew tribes were already in Palestine. This was especially true of the southern and northern sections. We read in the book of Joshua about covenants or treaties with tribes who had been in the land (Joshua 9; 14:6-15).

All the tribes are united at a covenant ceremony which is recorded in Joshua 24. Here Joshua recites what God has done (24:2-13) and then challenges the assembled tribes to swear allegiance to Jahweh. As they do, we have the formation of a 12-tribe nation united by a common allegiance to Jahweh.

Only by implication does the book of Joshua say that all the towns of Palestine were captured at this time. Actually Joshua records the capture of only a few towns in the central area, and these are smaller hill towns.

We are explicitly told that many parts of Palestine were not conquered (Joshua 13:1-13; Judges 1:16-36). This agrees quite well with what we know apart from the Bible. Archeological investigation shows an upheaval in central Palestine about 1200 B.C. It seems to have started in the central area and moved into the hill country just north and south of Jerusalem (see map 3).

Portions of the book of Joshua seem to imply that everyone ("all that breathed") was killed by the armies of Jahweh (Joshua 10:40). In fact, it was said that God so arranged it that no mercy would be shown and every Canaanite would be utterly destroyed (Joshua 11:20). This too is an implication which does not correspond to the description we find elsewhere in the Old Testament. The entire book of Judges presupposes a situation in which the Canaanites and the Israelites lived side by side and were involved in a long struggle to see who could hold the land.

Taking the country by storm?

Why then the constant implication that Joshua took the whole country by storm — killing everything in sight? To answer this leads us directly into the nature of the historical books of the Old Testament.

We are now beginning to study a section of the Bible called the Former Prophets (Joshua, Judges, 1 and 2 Samuel, 1 and 2 Kings). It covers the historical period from the conquest of Palestine, 1200 B.C., to the fall of the southern kingdom in 587 B.C. It is not a record of that period. The editor, called the Deuteronomist, makes that clear when he refers us to the archives — if we want "records" (1 Kings 11:41). The books of the Former Prophets were put together or edited by a person who had several "axes to grind":

1. He thought Jerusalem was the place designated by God for worship. Any other place was a violation of God's will.

2. He believed that the true "blessing" of Jahweh resided with the Davidic king. Other kings were an abomination to God.

3. He believed that history proceeded from the Word of God which is made known to us by the prophet. Because of this the structure of these books follows a definite pattern: a prophet came out and announced what would happen. Subsequent narratives show how this prophecy came to be fulfilled.

There are two major sections of "promise and fulfillment": the story of David's rise to the throne (1 Samuel 16 — 2 Samuel 5) and the story of a successor to the throne of David (2 Samuel 7 — 1 Kings 2). Within and around these two stories are a large number of smaller units each of which begins with a prophetic promise and ends with its fulfillment in Israel's history.

When was this history written? Shortly after the fall of Samaria (722/21 B.C.) someone tried to show that if Israel were to do as God willed it would have to regularize its worship by making Jerusalem the only legitimate place to celebrate the major festivals; it would have to restore the Davidic kingdom by holding all of Palestine under a "son of David"; it would have to drive out worshipers of Baal and other idolaters.

To create enthusiasm for this point of view, the book of Deuteronomy was written. The historical proof for this thesis was set forth in the Former Prophets, a set of books scholars now call the Deuteronomic historical books.

So these historical books try to show that God's promise to Abraham was fulfilled: After the exodus the promised land was given over to the Israelites and there were no worshipers of Baal anywhere in the country (Joshua 1 — 14). The entire area of Palestine was then divided (see map 4) so that each tribe and family had its share (Joshua 15 — 22). This structure was then consummated as an everlasting covenant (Joshua 23 — 24).

The Deuteronomist felt that Israel fell because she did not keep the idol worshipers out but allowed worship to take place in haphazard ways around the countryside. This caused the split of the kingdom and the fall of the Davidic empire.

The purpose of the Deuteronomist was to call the people of his time to do as was intended from the beginning and claim the entire kingdom which was rightfully theirs. For this reason the conquests recorded in Joshua seem much more drastic than was actually the case. God did fulfill his promise and we should claim it once more, said the editor.

For the Israelites, new in the land, there were several problems which became a life-and-death struggle for them. We might categorize them into three parts:

1. *Religion.* The Israelites were bound together under the name of Jahweh. Jahweh was a nomadic god, or at best a hill god (1 Kings 20:23, 28). What did he know about raising grain and grapes? In those days people believed that each god had a certain region under his control. It would be foolhardy to worship a god whose region was other than the one you lived in — especially if that were a desert and you were trying to raise crops!

The people around the Israelites worshiped their own local god — called their Baal. Each small area had its own Baal who was responsible for the crops of that region. Could the Hebrew people remain true to Jahweh in the face of possible economic failure? The answer was plain and simple: No. The situation was so bad by the time of Gideon that he had to worship Jahweh at night for fear of his Hebrew neighbors (Judges 6:27)! The problem of idolatry and of alienation from Jahweh brought about the destruction of Israel.

2. *Social consistency.* Every special group has problems with acculturation (the process of acquiring cultural traits and values from another group). The 12 tribes were no exception. As they lived beside the more urbane Canaanites they began to act and think as their neighbors did. Their concept of justice moved from one of keeping the covenant to one of "do all you can within the law."

The problems of acculturation were especially severe when Hebrews married persons from neighboring tribes. Joshua warned what would happen (23:12f.), and we note time and time again that it was foreign wives that caused Israel trouble (1 Kings 11:1-5; 16:31). At the end Ezra and Nehemiah forbade the Jews to marry outside their own ranks (Ezra 10:1-4).

The problem of intermarriage was especially acute

Prisoners from Ramses III's foreign conquests include neighbors of the Hebrews in Canaan. Shown from the left are Libyan, Semite, Hittite, Philistine, and Semite

A Canaanite god in
bronze covered in gold
leaf is typical of the
idols used by the
tribes living side by
side with the Hebrews

Courtesy of the
Oriental Institute
University of Chicago

because sex and religion were so intertwined in Canaanite culture. The local religion was what we call a nature religion, *e.g.*, its worship followed natural events. At the head of the Canaanite divine family was the god El (singular form of the Hebrew word for God, *Elohim*). His "son" was the local ruling god called Baal (master, husband, or lord). Baal is usually pictured as a storm god or as a bull — both symbolized fertility.

Every year as the rainy season began, Baal would defeat the god of death and sterility, Mot, thereby insuring a year of good crops. The conclusion of this ceremony was a sacred marriage between Baal and his consort, Asherah (Judges 3:7; 6:25). This marriage (carried out in practice by the king and a priestess) would cause the earth also to be fertile. The more "marriages" the better.

Naturally, then, the worship of the Canaanite was a sexual relationship, with the priestesses acting as sacred prostitutes. Needless to say, the more austere worship of Jahweh had a hard time competing with this type of religious service!

The book of Judges deals with this initial period in the life of Israel when the cause of Jahweh seemed to be all but lost.

3. *Political structure.* To this point our thesis has been that Israel was not a nation as such until the covenant of Shechem (Joshua 24), by which the tribes were bound together under the leadership of Jahweh. But who was the human leader? During the period of the Judges various men (and Deborah) were aroused by the spirit of Jahweh to lead a tribe or tribes into battle or otherwise manage their social life (we call these men charismatic — gifted). Such a system hardly would prove satisfactory for a nation of any size.

Therefore the Israelites were under constant pressure

to adopt the monarchical system of their neighbors. Normally speaking, there was nothing wrong with this, but for them to do so would deny the kingship of Jahweh and probably would lead to the royal excesses and idolatry which were also a part of the neighboring monarchies.

This is exactly what happened, but still the editor of Judges felt that the tribes needed a king (Davidic, of course). His last phrase indicates his opinion: "In those days there was no king in Israel; every man did what was right in his own eyes" (Judges 21:25).

These then are the crucial problems of Israel. We will try to illustrate them throughout our discussion of the Old Testament and particularly in the rest of this chapter. The story of how Joshua "fit the battle of Jericho," in Joshua 6, shows how Jahweh gave the land to the people. The other story, that of Samson in Judges 13 – 16, shows some of the problems which the Israelites faced in their new country and how often they failed to keep themselves loyal to Jahweh.

The trumpet of the Lord

MICROVIEW 5a
Joshua 6

In a Broadway play, Paddy Chayefsky has given us a fascinating interpretation of Gideon. He takes Gideon to be a real country hick, the least of the sons of Israel as far as intelligence and bravado are concerned. In a charming scene Jahweh comes to Gideon and proposes that he lead the tribes into battle against the marauding Midianites. Gideon is flattered and asks why he should be chosen. What is it that God sees in him? Jahweh replies that he wants to impress upon the Israelites that it was he who saved them. Therefore he chose the biggest lout in all Israel. If Gideon leads them to victory it must be God who saves them!

In many respects this is the theme of Joshua and Judges. Victory comes from the least-expected places.

One of the most startling and incredible stories is the taking of Jericho. Jericho was the strategic town for any invasion of Palestine from the east. It stood just across the Jordan River and guarded the major routes into the central hill territory. Because of its major importance and because it was the first victory in the new land, it has a special role in the narrative of Joshua.

How was Jericho taken?

The conquest began even before the Israelites crossed the Jordan and the story reads like a modern spy thriller (Joshua 2). Joshua sent two intelligence agents into the city for reconnaissance purposes. Acting like two conventioneers, they looked over the defenses of the city and then visited a house of prostitution to check out local

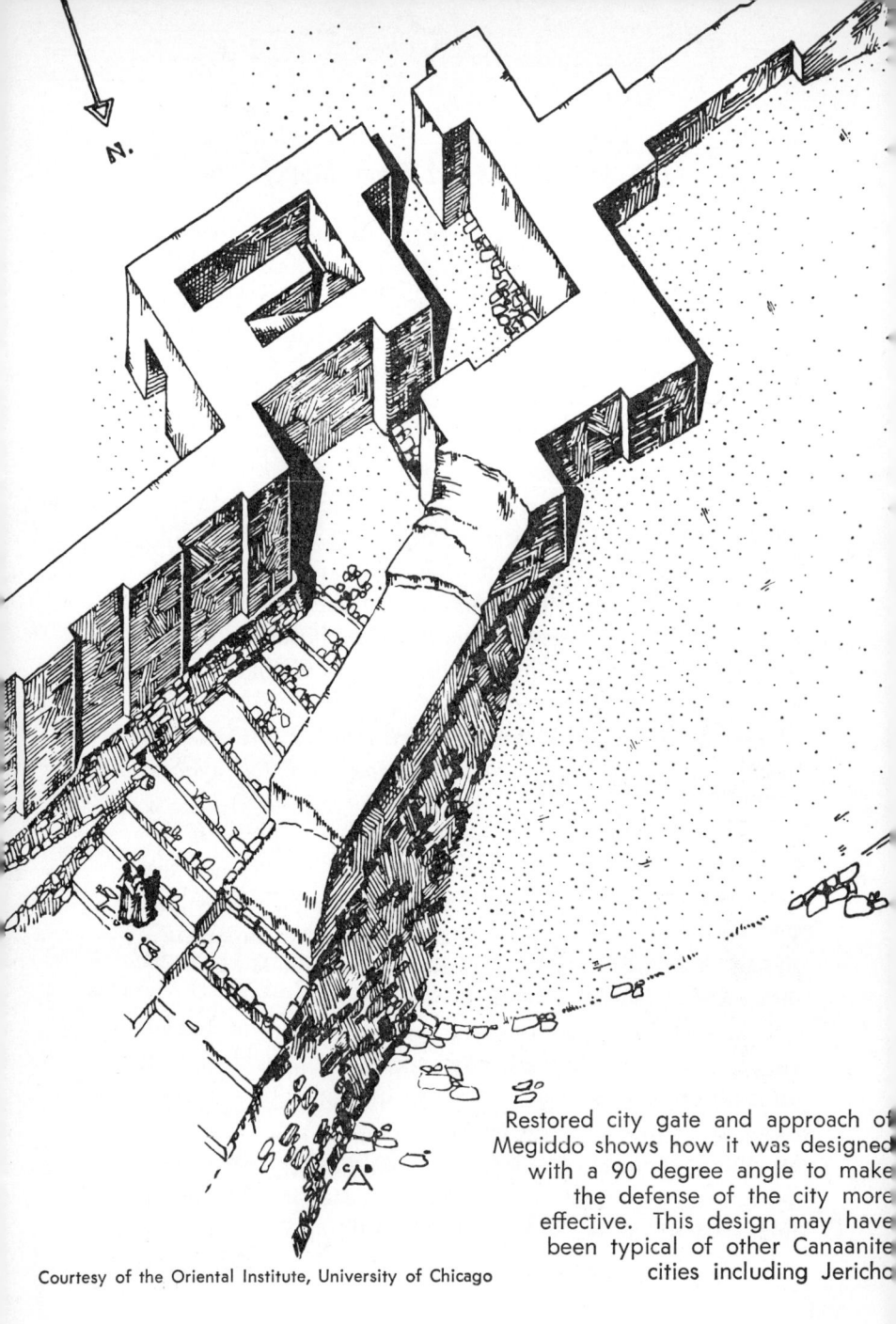

Restored city gate and approach of Megiddo shows how it was designed with a 90 degree angle to make the defense of the city more effective. This design may have been typical of other Canaanite cities including Jericho

Courtesy of the Oriental Institute, University of Chicago

morale. When darkness fell they needed to leave before the gates were closed for the night. But, as in any spy thriller, they were slow in leaving. The king's guard had heard of the Israelites and sent a squad over to the red-light district for the pickup. But Jericho had a saint (Hebrews 11:31) who hid the men in her penthouse. Who was the saint? Not the local priestess; not the local social actionist; not the local political rebel — but a prostitute. When the agents arrived, Rahab had a perfect story: "Oh, yes, there were a couple of men here, but after a few drinks they left by the side door and headed for the nearest city gate." The police headed for the ford of the Jordan River while Rahab went back up to her penthouse for a talk with her two guests.

Rahab confided to the spies that everyone was badly scared. They had heard of this Jahweh who had brought the Israelites out of Egypt and helped them destroy the kings of the Transjordan. Jericho didn't have a chance. Rahab ended her speech with a plea for mercy: She had saved them. Could they give her shelter when Jericho exploded?

Joshua's men agreed that one ought to give life for life and, if she would not inform on them, they would make sure that her home was not destroyed. In return she let them down the city wall by means of a rope. Back safely with Joshua, the men reported that Jericho had already lost the battle, psychologically at least.

Joshua then prepared for the attack. The Jordan crossing could be difficult, but once again Jahweh helped them through the water. This too impressed the Canaanites (5:1) and their spirits fell further. Meanwhile the Israelites prepared themselves religious-wise by undergoing circumcision and celebrating their first Passover in the promised land. Now they were ready for the attack.

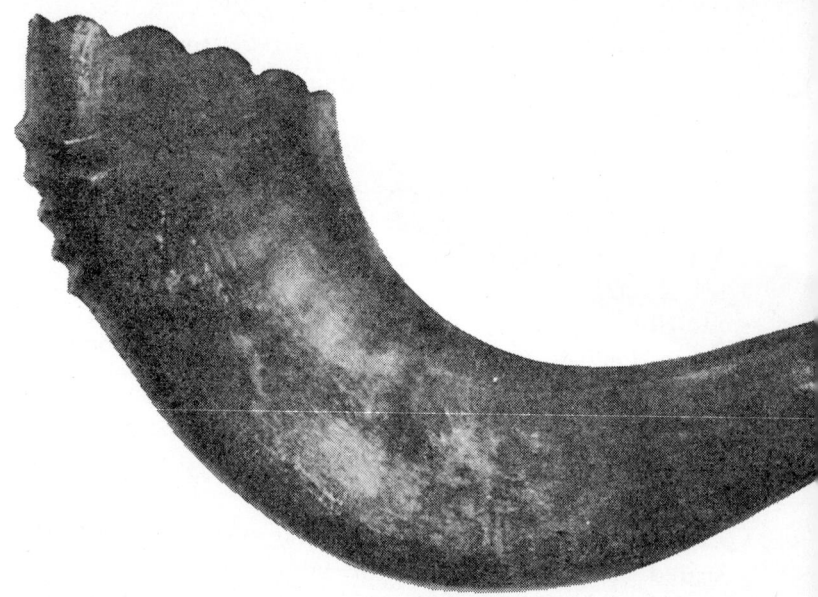

But instead of storming the walls with battering rams and scaling towers, they organized the entire army in parade dress, lined up the priests behind them, and followed with the ark on which Jahweh sat.

What is the importance of the ark?

In Arabic warfare it has been customary to take the prettiest girl of the tribe, place her on a traditional platform astride a camel, and lead her to a hill overlooking the scene of the battle. When the time came for the Arabs to charge, the girl would unloose her veil and her hair (women are always veiled in Arabic society). The sight of this flying hair on the beautiful girl was enough to make even the most weak-kneed Arab rush to the attack.

Some scholars think the platform is the counterpart of the ark. In the case of the Hebrews' ark of the covenant it was not a girl that rode on the platform, but Jahweh himself sitting on what we have come to call the

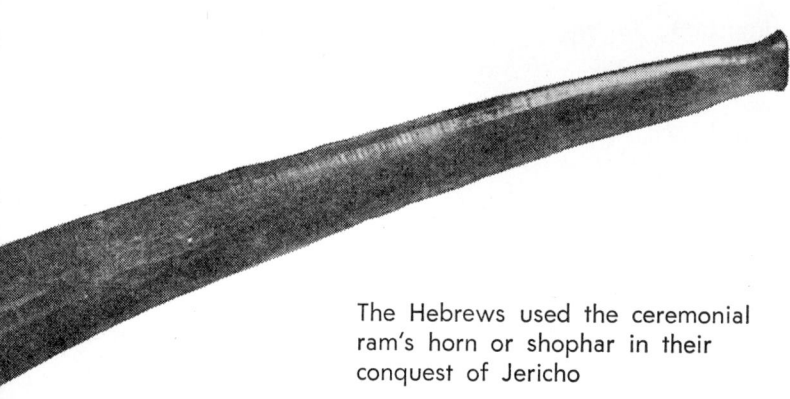

The Hebrews used the ceremonial ram's horn or shophar in their conquest of Jericho

Jewish Museum, N. Y. — Frank J. Darmstaedter Photo

"mercy seat." God was not physically represented as sitting there; it was only a seat for his presence.

Since warfare was religious in the ancient world, the presence of this platform with Jahweh's seat was no doubt demoralizing to an enemy army, as is attested in 1 Samuel 4:5-9.

For seven days the Hebrews marched around the walls of Jericho with great fanfare and trumpets in a religious procession. On the final day the suspense must have been fantastic. At any rate, when the people gave their final shout of triumph (perhaps the "Oh He" mentioned on page 76), Jericho collapsed and Jahweh triumphed without a shot. I have no doubt that many battles were won in just such a manner.

Yet we will not likely know just what happened at Jericho that spring when Joshua and his army conquered it. But again precise factual knowledge is not particularly important. Of more significance are the following two insights contained in the Jericho story:

1. The Hebrew people did not win Palestine on their own. *Even though Palestine might have been won by gradual infiltration, the tradition wishes to say that God gave the land to the Hebrew people.* This belief is crucial. It is to say that man does not accomplish the purposes of God. It is the same problem faced by Abraham in his attempts to get a son.

According to the theology of this account, whenever the kings tried to expand their kingdom or their power by their own might their attempts ended in failure. Isaiah says to Ahaz in 735 B.C.:

> If you will not believe,
> surely you will not be established.
>
> — *Isaiah 7:9*

This idea is the cornerstone of Jewish history. How often will the Hebrew shout: "The Lord has given them into the hand of Israel." As we shall see, it is the genius of David that he can so completely unite political expediency with the theological perception of God's power.

2. The priests play an important part in this story because it is the role of the priest to destroy walls. The walls of Jericho are barriers to the purpose of God and the destiny of his people. The priest is not a magician. The priest (or kingdom of priests) is on the cutting edge, leading the way against the barriers to God. Here at the first point of conquest it is a priestly victory, not a military one. Throughout their history the Israelites had to turn to the man of God for their focus. Not always is it the priest as such. Sometimes it is the prophet or the wise man. But in any case the way is paved by whoever has received God's word.

Faith, women, and idols

MICROVIEW 5b
Judges 13 — 16

Samson! The pride of Zorah! The man from Dan! Samson was a graduate of Zorah West High School with letters in all the sports. And was he ever handsome with that long hair! Some of the boys even tried to grow beards just like his, but it didn't seem to have the same effect. Still, the local barbers did a great business in the Samson-cut.

Samson was the only son of a rather peculiar couple over on the west side of Zorah. For many years this couple had not had any children, and in those days that was bad. It meant that the couple had no heirs to continue the family name. Because the Lord didn't give her any children, it was often whispered about that maybe Manoah's wife had done something terrible.

Anyway, this unusual family got the idea that the wife was going to have a son, who would be something special. He was going to be a Nazirite, a person who took a vow not to cut his hair or to drink wine. His mother started acting strangely even before he was born by refusing wine and avoiding all taboos.

It was a crazy way to act, for now that the Hebrews had come to live in Canaan things were different. Sure, they used to let their hair grow long, but now it was much more chic to do as the Canaanites did and shave every day. No one used to drink wine either, but now that the grapes were plentiful every family had a bottle of wine on the table. It was the thing to do. After all, one shouldn't be *too* different. How could one witness to other people about Jahweh if he were hindered by those quaint habits? Well, Samson's family was trying to live back in the "good old days" of the 1400's (B.C.) and their contemporaries of the 1200's thought their behavior was absurd.

You'll have to say this for his parents: they produced quite a boy. No one could match him or boss him around — not even his parents! They slipped at one essential point: they wouldn't let him cut his hair, they wouldn't let him drink wine — they should have made a monk out of him, too!

Women were his downfall. For some reason, perhaps because he grew up on the west side of town, he started going with the girls over in Timnah. Now you know what kind of people lived over in Timnah. Oh, some of them were nice all right, but they didn't worship Jahweh — they were Philistines.

It happened that Samson began to like one of the Timnah girls quite a bit. He had met her at a wild party, but he thought she was okay anyway. Well, Manoah and his wife were badly upset. Samson was the only son they had. They had expected big things of him among his own people. Now he wanted to marry one of *them*. They argued. Samson merely replied, "Go get her; I want her." No one argued with Samson — no one.

So Samson, Mom, and Dad went over to Timnah to make arrangements. Running on ahead of them, Samson bumped into a stray lion. The lion tried to attack him and was torn limb from limb by the barehanded Samson. A short while later, the marriage arrangements were made.

On another visit Samson passed the body of the lion he had mauled. In it was a swarm of bees. Reaching in, he took some of the honey and kept a bit for his parents.

The wedding day came. Dad and Samson went down the valley to Timnah for the feast. His own friends would

An ivory inlay from Megiddo depicts a Canaanite girl of Samson's time

Courtesy of the Oriental Institute, University of Chicago

have nothing to do with this "mixed marriage"; so the big-hearted Philistines gave him 30 young men to be his "friends" for the week. In those days they used to tell riddles to one another much as we play games at a party. So Samson gave the boys a riddle and a wager to go with it. The wager was a good one: "If you guess before the week is up I'll pay for the tuxedos; if you don't guess it you pay for the tuxedos." The riddle was:

> Out of the eater came something to eat.
> Out of the strong came something sweet.

Well, the Philistine boys were not very bright and they couldn't make any sense out of this riddle. Finally their national pride caught up with them and they approached the bride. "Look," they said, "you brought us over here to do a favor for you and now that Samson will ruin us all because we can't get the answer to his riddle. You get the answer."

The young bride was reluctant, but she turned on the tears before the bridegroom and the naive Samson finally told her the answer. So on the seventh day, just as the sun was going down, the Philistine boys came up with a sly reply:

> What is sweeter than honey?
> What is stronger than a lion?

Samson was fast on the draw, too. He saw what had happened and whipped back a bit of poetry:

> If you had not plowed with my heifer,
> you would not have found out my riddle.

He was so burned up that he rushed to the main street of Ashkelon, 20 miles away, killed the first 30 men he saw, took their tuxedos from them. With these borrowed items he paid off the wager.

Still hot under the collar, Samson returned to Zorah for a cooling-off period. Somewhat pacified at last, he returned to Timnah with a "kiss and makeup" gift for his wife. His father-in-law met him and informed him that his wife was given to the best man, since they figured that Samson would never come back.

"Now don't get angry, Samson," the frightened father-in-law said. "You are welcome to her little sister. She's better looking anyway."

Samson was in no mood for little sisters. He caught 300 foxes, then made 150 torches and tied them to the tails of 150 pairs of foxes. This holocaust almost destroyed the entire Philistine wheat crop. When the Philistines attempted a reprisal, Samson killed 1,000 of them with a bone.

After all this, Samson seemed not to have learned his lesson. Over at the big city of Gaza he met another Philistine girl and started dating her. One night the Gazites figured that they would get him about dawn, but Samson slipped out the east gate. On the way out he decided to take the gate with him as a souvenir and carried it almost 40 miles to Hebron!

The third Philistina was too much for him. In Delilah he met his match. After he had gone with her for a while, the chief of state came in secret and managed to persuade her to use her charms in a constructive manner — find out the secret of Samson's strength. "Oh, yes, we'll give you some hard cash for your great beauty," he promised. Well, Samson and Delilah carried on a delightful game of cat and mouse. Samson sent her on the wildest of goose chases: hunting up freshly dried cat-gut, dandelion chains, and all sorts of mysterious things. Each time Samson escaped and laughed at his puzzled opponents.

But the woman won (she always does in these stories).

He finally told her of his vow, and that his hair was the secret of his strength. That evening he fell asleep on her lap — a tender and touching scene! The local barber rushed in and performed the operation.

This time the shave was too close and Samson was easy prey for the Philistine militia. They caught him, gouged out his eyes, and in a most humiliating fashion made the star of Zorah push a millwheel.

What an end to such a promising young man! His hair *was* odd, but it was his virility, his manhood, his strength. When he was barbered he looked like any other clean-shaven "feminine" Canaanite. His vow was broken; his manliness left him; he was acculturized!

Samson made one mistake: women. The Philistines made another. They forgot the cause for Samson's great strength. They failed to send around a barber and keep him shaved. His strength came back.

Samson said nothing of his renewed power and gave no hint it had returned. Then the right day came. At a great festival for their own god — a festival no doubt like the ones at which he had met his girl friends — the Philistines rejoiced in their victory over Samson. He was brought in for their entertainment. He heard their laughs and jeers. He heard the familiar fun-making. Pretending to be faint, he asked the boy who was his "eye" to take him to the pillars of the temple. There being 3,000 of the Philistine faithful present on this occasion, Samson said to himself, "Well, 3,000 aren't much, but they'll avenge one of my eyes at least."

With a prayer to Jahweh, he grabbed the two pillars and with one great heave destroyed the temple and all in it.

Appendix

CHRONOLOGICAL TABLE

Dates	Events and Persons	Bible
	Creation	Genesis 1-2
	Adam and Eve	Genesis 2-3
	Cain and Abel	Genesis 4
	The Flood	Genesis 6-9
	Tower of Babel	Genesis 11
2000	Amorite invasion	
ca. 1650	Migration to Canaan	Genesis 12
	Abraham, Isaac, Jacob	Genesis 12-36
ca. 1370	Hebrews enter Egypt	
	Joseph	Genesis 37-50
ca. 1220	Exodus	
	Call to Moses	Exodus 3-4
	The Passover	Exodus 11-13
	Red Sea deliverance	Exodus 14
	Ten Commandments	Exodus 20
	Covenant ceremony	Exodus 24
	Conquest of Canaan	Joshua
	Joshua	
ca. 1200	Fall of Jericho	Joshua 6
1200-1020	Period of the Judges	Judges
	Deborah	Judges 4-5
	Gideon	Judges 6-8
	Samson	Judges 14-16

THE KINGDOM OF ISRAEL

1020-1000	Saul, first king	1 Samuel 8-13
1000-961	David, second king	1 Samuel 16 – 2 Samuel
961-922	Solomon, third king	1 Kings 1-11
922	Kingdom divides	
	Judah (Southern Kingdom)	
	Israel (Northern Kingdom)	

	JUDAH	ISRAEL	
922-915	Rehoboam		1 Kings 12-14
922-901		Jeroboam	1 Kings 12-14
913-873	Asa		1 Kings 15
873-849	Jehoshaphat		1 Kings 22
869-850		Ahab	1 Kings 16-22
		Elijah	
		Micaiah	
		Elisha	2 Kings 2-13
842-815		Jehu	2 Kings 9-10
837-800	Jehoash		2 Kings 11-12
800-783	Amaziah		2 Kings 14
786-746		Jeroboam II	2 Kings 14
750		Amos	Amos
745		Hosea	Hosea
783-742	Uzziah		2 Kings 15
735-715	Ahaz		2 Kings 16-17
742-700	Isaiah		Isaiah 1-39
	Micah		Micah
722-21		Israel falls to Assyrians	2 Kings 17

END OF NORTHERN KINGDOM

JUDAH

715-687	Hezekiah	2 Kings 18-20
687-642	Manasseh	2 Kings 21
640-609	Josiah (Deuteronomic reform)	2 Kings 22-23
628-580	Jeremiah	Jeremiah
598-571	Ezekiel	Ezekiel
587	Judah falls to Babylonians	2 Kings 24-25

END OF SOUTHERN KINGDOM

587-538	Period of exile	
	Second Isaiah	Isaiah 40-55
539	Edict of Cyrus	
538	Return of exiles	
520-515	Rebuilding of the temple	Ezra
	Zerubbabel	

445-433	Rebuilding of walls of Jerusalem Nehemiah	Nehemiah
ca. 427	The Law enforced . . . Ezra	
400-167	Jews under Persian, Greek, Egyptian, and Syrian domination	
	Jews resist reform . . .	Ruth Jonah Job
175-164	Antiochus Epiphanes . .	
167	Maccabean revolt . . .	
	Judas Maccabaeus . .	Daniel
164	Rededication of Temple . .	
164-63	Jews enjoy nominal freedom	
63	Pompey captures Jerusalem; beginning of Roman domination	
37-4	Herod the Great . . .	
30-14 A.D.	Augustus Caesar . . .	
6	Birth of Jesus	
A.D.		The Four
27	Baptism of Jesus . . .	Gospels
26-36	Pontius Pilate	
27-30	Ministry of Jesus . . .	
30	Crucifixion and resurrection of Jesus Christ	
30	Beginning of the Christian church . . .	Acts 2
33	Conversion of Paul . .	Acts 9
47	Jerusalem Council . .	Acts 15
47-64	Paul's missionary journeys	Acts Pauline letters
54-68	Nero	
70	Destruction of Jerusalem . .	
70-100?	The church faces the world	1 Peter Revelation

SURVEY OF BIBLICAL HISTORY
The Patriarchs to the Conquest of Palestine (1650-1200 B.C.)

We assume the general historical nature of the events described in this period but it is difficult to pinpoint any dates. The Patriarchs came from a wandering seminomadic people called Arameans. They lived in the desert near the settled areas and tried to gain a foothold from time to time. Abraham, Isaac, and Jacob were tribal fathers who tried to possess Palestine sometime between 1650 and 1400.

Some of these Arameans (called Hebrews) went down into Egypt, possibly about 1370, and there became a slave people under the Pharaohs. There was excessive brutality under one Pharaoh, Ramses II (1290-1224), and finally the Hebrews in Egypt, under the leadership of Moses, managed to escape during the rule of Ramses' successor, Merneptah (1224-1216). After a period in the wilderness or desert between Egypt and Palestine, these Hebrews managed to cross the Jordan River, take some major cities in the central part of Palestine, and join hands with fellow Hebrews who were already living in the area. Their leader, Moses, was succeeded by Joshua during this period.

The Rise of the Davidic Empire (1200-922 B.C.)

For a long period the Hebrew people lived side by side with the Canaanites and the Philistines, who also tried to possess the land. During this period they were ruled by various judges — men who became famous as "lawyers" and served as advisers on various problems that arose among the people. In times of stress there were also Spirit-filled men like Gideon and Samson who helped the Hebrews free themselves from foreign oppression. Eventually the Hebrew people felt a need for a more permanent ruler who would judge between them on important decisions and also would give them a permanent defense against their enemies. From this desire rose Saul (1020-1000), the first king over Israel.

Though a good king, Saul failed to satisfy everyone concerned and was succeeded by the great king David (1000-

961). David managed to bring all the tribes together into a national unity with Jerusalem as the capital city. He developed a strong army and not only protected Israel from her enemies but also conquered most of the surrounding nations. Furthermore, he developed the worship patterns and practices for succeeding centuries even to our day.

During this high period there was also a great deal of literary activity. Some of the basic portions of the Pentateuch (Genesis to Deuteronomy) were established as well as the beginning of proverbs and songs or psalms. David was followed by a wise son, Solomon (961-922), who turned out to be wiser in literature than in administration. At the end of his reign the kingdom split into two enemy factions (as they were before Saul united them). The south, ruled by Rehoboam (922-915), was called Judah and kept Jerusalem as its capital and center of worship. The north, ruled by Jeroboam (922-901), was called Israel and its capital was finally Samaria with worship centers at Bethel and Dan.

The Divided Kingdoms (922-587 B.C.)

The Northern Kingdom lacked the continuity of government and the clarity of purpose to remain a strong nation. It was the larger and stronger of the two kingdoms and in some respects closer to the original association of tribes during the period of the judges. But its history is one of steady decline. There was a long period of success under Omri and his family (876-842), but for the most part the times were filled with intrigue and revolt. The people themselves were greatly influenced by the worship of the Canaanites, and the nation strayed from the covenant originally set with Jahweh. Into this situation came the great prophets Elijah (*ca.* 850) and Elisha, who called the people to true worship.

Just before the end of its existence, Israel was enjoying a prosperous period under Jeroboam II (786-746). But moral decay had begun. Two prophets, Amos and Hosea (750-745), emerged at this time to warn of the coming tragedy — Israel would be destroyed and taken into captivity. These spokesmen for God were not heeded and the kings of Israel continued to plot with Syria against the ruling power of that time, Assyria. Provoked into war by the gadflies, Israel and Syria, the Assyrian kings rolled west with their armies and defeated the two kingdoms (732). But Israel was still not satisfied and once again revolted. This time the Assyrian power was merciless. Shalmaneser V and his son, Sargon II, thoroughly destroyed Samaria and took away the leaders of Israel into captivity (722). In turn, foreign elements were brought into Samaria and it was this mixed group which made up the Samaritans of the New Testament period.

Meanwhile, though weaker, Judah managed to stay alive. A Davidic king stayed on the throne despite several long periods of subjection to Assyria or Egypt. At the time of Israel's revolt one of the truly great prophets, Isaiah of Jerusalem (742-700), warned King Ahaz (735-715) to remain aloof. Ahaz failed to heed the advice and invited Assyrian domination by his actions. His son Hezekiah (715-687) was more sympathetic to Isaiah and tried to liberate Judah from Assyria and her system (including her gods). Assyria again marched west to quell the revolt and Jerusalem was taken or besieged by Sennacherib (705-681) in 701. Judah remained quiet for several years even to the point of turning away from Jahweh under Manasseh (687-642).

But under the brilliant leadership of King Josiah (640-609), worship of Jahweh was restored, the cult was centralized and reformed, and the Davidic empire was regained to some extent. This time Assyria was so threatened by the rising Babylonian power that she could not stop this revolt. Hebrew hopes rose with Josiah and just as the international struggle looked good for Judah, Josiah was killed at Megiddo (609) while trying to cut off Egyptian aid to Assyria. In 605 King Nebuchadrezzar (605-562) of Babylonia conquered Assyria and made Judah a vassal kingdom. A great prophet, Jeremiah (*ca.* 628-587), had been watching all this and warned that Judah would end up as Israel had. But Judah believed that she was divinely protected and plunged on to her doom. She revolted against Babylonia and was defeated by Nebuchadrezzar in 597. Once again Judah tried to gain freedom and, like Israel, was thoroughly destroyed and sent into captivity (587).

The Exile and the Restoration (587-400 B.C.)

The Hebrews had been warned of the catastrophe by the prophet Ezekiel (598-571) and now that it had come he helped them reconstruct their life in Babylonia. But great changes were in store for the Near East. The Babylonian Empire was not strong and by 545 it was apparent that Cyrus of Persia (550-530) would soon destroy it. The Hebrew people rejoiced in their coming liberator and looked forward to restoring their Davidic kingdom back in Palestine. One prophet understood that all this happened so that the nations and peoples of the world might be brought by Judah back to fellowship with God. We do not know his name but we have his profound poems in Isaiah 40-55.

Babylonia did fall to Cyrus in 540 and by edict of the new ruler the Jews were free to return to Palestine (*ca.* 538). Life was not easy in the destroyed country. Houses and cities had to be rebuilt and enemies were everywhere. Finally two prophets, Haggai and Zechariah (520-515), called the people to rebuild the temple. It was completed in 515. Still the community did not advance and in 445 Nehemiah arrived to organize the little group into a religious state ruled by the priestly class. Some time later, Ezra (427 ?) arrived to establish the religious laws of the community along lines now found in the Pentateuch, especially Leviticus.

The Intertestamental Period (400-6 B.C.)

The Persian Empire was destroyed by the Greek Alexander the Great in 333. Alexander died in 323 and the Near East was eventually split between two factions: the Seleucids in Syria and the Ptolemies in Egypt. A particularly eager and hated Seleucid emperor, Antiochus Epiphanes (175-164), tried to hellenize (convert from Judaism) the population of Palestine completely. Because of this intense pressure the Jews revolted under the Maccabeans in 167. Antiochus was enraged and sought to destroy the Jews. In the face of this onslaught a writer encouraged his fellow Jews to have courage. His book is known to us as Daniel. Judas Maccabeus managed to hold off the Seleucids and after Antiochus' death the Jews managed to keep nominal independence until 63, when the Roman Empire invaded the Near East. Jerusalem was taken by Pompey and Palestine remained subject to Rome until well past the end of the New Testament period.

The Beginning of the Church

Rome turned the management of the Jews over to a Near Eastern family called the Herods. Herod the Great ruled until 4 B.C. with relative success. Before Herod's death, Jesus of Nazareth was born (6 B.C.). Following the death of Herod the Great, Palestine was ruled by several of the Herod family under Roman supervision. After this arrangement failed, Judea, at least, became a Roman province under direct rule of Rome by a procurator. Chief of these for New Testament history was Pontius Pilate (26-36) under whom Jesus was crucified (33). The resurrection of Jesus was followed by the beginning of the church in Jerusalem and the conversion of Paul (30). While the Jerusalem church was working with the Jews, Paul was preparing for a great mission to the Gentiles. At the crucial council of Jerusalem (47) the decision was made to undertake this mission. The letters of Paul resulted from this missionary work and the development of basic traditions resulted in the formation of a "gospel," Mark (65).

In Jerusalem the threat of persecution and the coming revolt of the Jews against Rome forced the Christians to leave in 67. The destruction of Jerusalem by Titus in 70 destroyed the final organic connection of Christianity with Judaism. Following the destruction of Jerusalem the church was deeply involved with its mission, with increased persecution from Roman and local authorities, and with dissension in her ranks. From this time until the end of the first century we have various documents dealing with these problems. They comprise our New Testament.